Zimmer Gunsul Frasca Partnership

Preface by
Robert J. Frasca, FAIA
Introduction by
Allan Temko

Between Science and Art

Editorial Director USA
Pierantonio Giacoppo

Chief Editor of Collection
Maurizio Vitta

Publishing Coordinator
Franca Rottola

Graphic Design
Paola Polastri

Editing
Martyn J. Anderson

Colour-separation
Litofilms Italia, Bergamo

Printing
Poligrafiche Bolis, Bergamo

First published December 1998

ISBN 88-7838-052-0

Contents

Foreword

by Robert J. Frasca, FAIA

The work represented here focuses on our efforts of the past five years and at this printing exists in various forms of completion. In some cases, the projects have literally been torn from the drafting table (or more commonly the computer) unfinished even in the development of the idea but indicative of our fundamental intentions. In others, the work exists as a gigantic excavation with only the foundations to map what will soon leave its full thumbprint on its surroundings. In the third case, the work is near completion, not quite ready for prime time display but its qualities are evident even in an unadorned state. Finally, there are the projects that are in use, have been animated and tested by their inhabitants, so the true value can be assessed. For us it is valuable to look at a generation of work in this telephoto fashion and in the various stages of completion. The exercise is not only a test of one's own convictions over time but also helps detect glacial shifts from one generation of work to the next that are brought about by external forces.

The fundamental premise that unites all our work is that architecture in addition to being a visual art is a social one and it varies with time, place and traditions of the people who use it. It is the instincts of the architect first as observer and then as builder that determines the quality and validity of the final result. How this body of work stands up to this litmus test is ultimately the obligation of the reader.

However, I believe it is useful to give a personal overview that will provide a framework for a critical evaluation.

We continue to be involved in the broadest spectrum of the built environment with the conviction that one building type informs another as well as for the pure joy of it. The specifics of what gives each building its form is the indefinable alchemy that takes place between architect, client and place at a particular point in time. It goes without saying that a variation of any one of these ingredients would certainly produce a very different result. The examples that follow will briefly explain the work in these terms.

College and university planning and design have been a particularly engaging part of our practice. Williams College and Reed College, at opposite ends of the continent, struggle with a similar issue; that being the need to provide for change while trying to stay the same. Both projects deal with weaving additions onto existing buildings located in cherished places on a finely-scaled campus. Both solutions strive to reinforce a sense of community in a seamless way so that change will not conflict with the traditions that for them hold incredible value.

The corporate campuses included here have similar motives but being built from whole cloth, deal with traditions that are not wholly-formed, are continually evolving at a rapid pace, and are measured in months or years rather than decades or centuries.

Each, however, still reflects the values of the people who work there and the ethic of the institution at that point in time. From the design standpoint, the ethic is egalitarian and as a result individual buildings are secondary to a preeminent landscape.

The single exception and the only important place in the hierarchy is the company cafeteria.

The opportunities to build for those involved with care and cure of human disease have been gratifying. In this somewhat neglected segment of the built environment, the doctors, researchers and patients we encounter value the qualities in building that nurture the human spirit as much as the specific functional requirements that often drive the design of the places in which they work. The Doernbecher Children's Hospital is a case in point.

The location of the hospital (or more accurately the air rights) was determined by the necessity to connect to existing programs located on either side of a canyon. While the site suggested one formal image, the quality for the interior wanted to be quite another. Therefore, the building form "plays big" in a powerful landscape, but the interior "plays small". Courtyards surrounded by patient rooms have the ambiance of a small European hotel, and the colors and detail are directed to the children who are in residence.

The expansion to the Clinical Research Center at the National Institutes of Health is similar in its mission but carries the additional responsibility of integrating the existing into a new order that will be defined by this new addition.

The validity of the solution will be determined by how well the addition contributes to quality of life of the whole. Because of the enormous size of the expanded complex, clarity and an obvious hierarchy with visual connections to the outdoors were essential to accomplish this goal.

We continue to concentrate our energies on work that touches many aspects of urban life. The experience with the California Science Center and the master plan for Exposition Park that preceded it was one of the most rewarding in memory from several standpoints. Some of us who initiated its design are from the generation that entered the profession with the expectation that altering the built environment was useful in affecting social ills. The program for the Science Center was one of the first that was initiated to revitalize south central Los Angeles after it had been ravaged by the Rodney King riots. Soon after the opening, we watched the quarter mile long line of families, four abreast, waiting to enter the museum. They represented an almost perfect cross section of the multicultural neighborhoods surrounding the park. It would have made the most cynical elitist misty eyed.

It has been our experience that infrastructure is a potent determinant in transforming urban form both from the standpoint of redefining existing areas and directing suburban growth.

Now nearing completion, the west side extension to the Portland light rail (MAX) continues the eastern corridor we completed earlier in the decade.

The three new stations shown here promise to dignify the area they serve and in some cases in ways that were not anticipated at the outset. Having made a visible connection to the fringe of the downtown, the image of the city's center is being expanded with new and complementary activities.

The Washington Park Station, which is farther out, not only connects this activity with the metropolitan area but serves the surrounding residential areas.

The commercial office building has always been the mainstay of downtown development and probably more than any other building type is a direct reflection of the sensibilities of the

marketplace at the time it is built.

Only as this decade draws to a close have new office towers begun to rise with any degree of regularity on the American skyline. The ones we are currently involved in put an even greater emphasis on the public realm than before but are directed more by economic constraints than stylistic predilections of the owner or architect than they have been in the past.

Lastly, the most unique program we have encountered in this time frame is for the Assembly Building for the Church of Jesus Christ of Latter-day Saints in the center of Salt Lake City. Founded by church members 150 years ago, the city is conspicuous on our continent in that its central focus, Temple Square, is also the headquarters for a worldwide church. Now in construction, the project's principal component is a worship space seating 21,000 people. Tucked into a sloping site, the ten-acre building footprint is overlaid with a park which extends the adjacent Temple Square and honors the Temple as the center piece of the now two-block complex of parks and buildings. The architectural vocabulary of church architecture has been deeply rooted in their traditions. It required us to translate across the one and one-half centuries they have been building in the Salt Lake Valley with an urban structure and room of a magnitude that to our knowledge had never been attempted before.

In summary, as we look back on this generation of work, it has much in common with the previous one in a few major respects. The first is that we continue to believe that by design, potentially divergent elements of a community can find common ground. So much of what we do draws its

inspiration from the surroundings and the people who will use it. Secondly it has always been more important for us to build well rather than be stylistically ambitious. Therefore the craft of how we make buildings continues to preoccupy us.

If there is one element that is different now it is that the tools of our trade have changed more rapidly in this past generation of work.

The computer enables us to see things in ways that we were never able to before but it has not altered the buildings any more than the word processor has the written word.

We continue to work with our clients in such a way that they can intervene in the design process in constructive ways and in all cases it has been with those whose motives are similar to our own. That is something that will never change.

Between Science and Art

by Allan Temko

Allan Temko, *the Architecture Critic for the "San Francisco Chronicle" for many years, was the recipient of the Pulitzer Prize for Criticism in 1990.*

Small may be beautiful, but bigness has been even better for Zimmer Gunsul Frasca. Within a single decade, starting at the end of the 1980s, ZGF has been transformed from a Northwest regionalist office of 70 or 80 people, perfectly at home in Portland, Oregon, into a 300-person nationwide organization with branches in Seattle, Los Angeles, and Washington, D.C. What is astonishing in this expansion has not been its speed but ZGF's continued high quality of design.

Other firms have grown as rapidly, usually with unfortunate architectural results, whereas ZGF has gone big without any slackening of aesthetic and social conviction. Its work, if anything, is richer and more profound, as commissions come in to remake rather large chunks of cities, such as the 21,000-seat Assembly Hall for the Church of Jesus Christ of Latter-day Saints in downtown Salt Lake City.

This will be one of the largest mostly underground rooms in the world for religious worship, many times more spacious than the crypt at Lourdes. In the pragmatic American way, however, the vast auditorium will also serve as a theater for religious pageants. Roofed by a terraced park, enlivened by a waterfall and monumental stairs, open day and night, the 10-acre site – presently underutilized – will become a landscaped amenity that will effectively double the size of Temple Square, the central gathering place for Mormons from all over the world.

Yet, if the magnificent stone-hewn Mormon Temple of the last century is closed except to members of the Church, the Assembly Hall and especially its rooftop park will welcome people of all backgrounds and beliefs.

Quite literally, it will be a testament of pluralism, and therefore, not a conventional isolated building at all, but rather a landscaped continuum, lodged in the slope of a low hill, which could advance through a downtown that sorely needs to be knitted together and refreshed by gardens. As a model for the future, it should be one of the first great "green" environments of the next century.

Nevertheless the forward-looking concept also hearkens back to High Modern idealism of a generation or two ago, to Kevin's Roche's Oakland Museum, say, or to Arthur Erickson's visionary superblock of law courts and government offices in Vancouver, B.C., topped by space-frame greenhouses.

The architecture also reflects lessons in city-building by the urban theorist, Kevin Lynch, which Robert J. Frasca, design partner of ZGF, learned at MIT.

Still another influence was that of Pietro Belluschi, architecture dean at MIT, who first brought truly Modern architecture to Portland and encouraged Frasca to settle there in the 1950s. But first Frasca received a traveling fellowship to Europe, including a visit to ancestral Italy (a liberal architectural education in itself) and several months in Finland, where he came to know Alvar Aalto's buildings by heart.

All this was part of the making of a firm whose humane outlook unites what otherwise might seem an array of unrelated buildings in various parts of the country, serving different purposes. In the last few years alone, ZGF has done hospitals and other health facilities, bio-tech labs and science museums, Federal courts and offices, downtown offices and a trade center, academic buildings on campuses as widely separated as Reed College in Portland, Williams College in Massachusetts, and the University of California at Santa Barbara, plus the enlargement of Portland's burgeoning international airport and a new line of the light-rail transit system, one of the finest anywhere, which links up with ZGF's exhilarating and beautifully planned convention center.

Whether Frasca or partners Greg Baldwin in Portland, Doss Mabe in Los Angeles or Evett Ruffcorn in Seattle are the principal designer of these projects, each of these different buildings possesses a local veracity.

It is true to its site and historical context, its functional or spiritual purpose, and above all the psychological as well as the physical needs of the individuals who actually live and work in them.

But there is no single truth for all of them. There is only a shared set of principles, applicable anywhere, but by their very nature undogmatic and non-egotistical. By paradox, since ZGF is no longer strictly a regional firm, these principles may define a new regionalism, a higher regionalism, that goes beyond traditional limits of geography. To Frasca himself, following the great example of Aalto, but now on a larger scale, regionalism has never been a preconceived historical style, such as the Spanish Colonial stageset of Santa Barbara. Instead, it is a process or method – what Eero Saarinen called "problem-solving" – which precludes uniformity and pictorialism when problems are solved correctly.

Somehow, by gentle precept and example, this spirit of the firm – founded 35 years ago by the late Norm Zimmer, who took care of the business, with Frasca, and Brooks

Gunsul, an excellent technician – has been imparted in virtually everything ZGF has done. In the last two decades, Frasca, complemented by his colleagues Robert Packard, Dan Huberty, and Larry Bruton, on the business and technical sides, has redesigned ZGF as the practice has widened, keeping the hands-on feeling of a smaller, more intimate office as the next generation of firm leadership (including newer partners Randy Leach, Ken Sanders, and Karl Sonnenberg) pushes forward into the '90s.

Hence ZGF has become a new kind of architectural practice, without losing touch with its origins.

Continuity combines with innovation in a building as boldly conceived as the Doernbecher Children's Hospital, spanning a ravine on its wooded site overlooking Portland. Here the architects were inspired by a program at the leading edge of medical science. The new chief of pediatrics, Dr. Ronald Rosenberg, came to Oregon from the famous children's hospital at Stanford University; and thanks mainly to him, virtually all significant recent developments in children's health care, psychological as well as physical, such as the special consideration given to parents who may stay overnight or prepare food for their very sick children, have been translated by ZGF into architecture of rare compassion and grace.

Taken as environment alone, it is probably the best children's hospital ever built. The bridge-like structure, 480 feet long on its topmost levels, literally ties together hitherto separate parts of Oregon Health Sciences University. The campus may be

charitably described as one of the worst planned, or rather unplanned, medical centers in the country (although it is near the top academically); and in the last decade, valiant efforts have been made to tie it all together.

The Children's Hospital, however, required so much space on the campus that the architects – taking a lesson from Frank Lloyd Wright – saw the chance to use a seemingly unbuildable location – a steep ravine – thereby freeing the surrounding slopes as a natural setting for the children to see and enjoy. Wherever views could be opened, to the distant snowy peaks of Mt. Hood, Mt. Adams, and Mt. St. Helen's, or to the downtown Portland cityscape, which ZGF has done so much to change over the last 20 years, the architects framed the perspectives in clear or fritted glass.

But at closer range they were also able to scale down the building to children's size, creating charming outdoor courts which Bob Frasca, remembering country inns in France, fitted with awnings and other playful features, down to the tiled pavings.

Artists, and even a poet, were brought into the conceptual process, something ZGF likes to do. The public reception areas were given a cordial, non-intimidating mood, almost domestic, although the building cannot escape a certain monumental quality because it is so large.

The exterior, sheathed in white metal panels that pick up the blue of the Oregon sky, presented comparable problems of scale. Nothing could make this hospital of 250,000 square feet look small, but rounded forms soften its overall impact, for instance the circular mechanical rooftop enclosures, which would have been ponderous if they were square.

Still more eloquent is the great curving facade, drawn into a long shallow arc across the full width of the building. If the geometry elsewhere sometimes recalls Le Corbusier's this majestic curtain wall of metal and glass seems to echo Erich Mendelsohn's expressionist drama of the 1920s.

This is not an altogether new theme for ZGF. A decade or so ago, the powerful curve of the Bonneville Power Administration Headquarters, perched above a Portland freeway, bore a clear resemblance to Mendelsohn's department store in Chemnitz.

But at the Children's Hospital the architecture is more accomplished.

The curve is no longer a formal device, fine as it was, but an outward expression of the inner life of the building.

In particular the pattern of circulation deserves analysis.

Two "streets" run through the clinical levels of the hospital: one a "public" thoroughfare, meant for families and visitors; the other an interior "service" corridor, the private realm of the patients and the staff.

In most hospitals, even well-designed new ones, public and private activities are often mingled, with patients and equipment being wheeled through conventional hallways. At Doernbecher that traffic problem has been solved.

The hospital is thus in many ways a paradigm of a small city, or at least a definable urbane community. ZGF's purpose, in Frasca's phrase, is "community-building"; and the firm strives, wherever possible, to multiply environmental dividends from a single investment.

Now, in referring to the masterly Modernist forerunners of ZGF's work – Saarinen and Aalto and Corbu, Mendelsohn and Wright – I wish only to point out how thoroughly their art has been assimilated in the ongoing architecture of a firm as distinguished as ZGF at the close of the 20th century.

Theirs is the vocabulary which the architectural poetry of the future will be written, constantly enriched by new generations of designers in an age of resistless technical and social change.

And that makes ZGF's blending of past and present. Sometimes, that goes beyond contextualism. Different periods are literally combined, almost locked together, as in the Unified Sciences Center at Williams College, at the expanded library and other buildings on the Reed College campus, or – more like a fusion than a simple addition – in the charming Peninsula Center Library at Palos Verdes, CA. Here ZGF enlarged and strengthened a decent building designed only 25 years ago by A. Quincy Jones, but unable to meet today's structural standards and community needs. Upscale Palos Verdes, a comely place, required a higher civic image, as well as a much better library. As in many affluent suburbs, all this was to be provided on a relatively modest budget.

The result is an ingenious interweaving of earlier and later work, most apparent in the main reading room, now doubled in size, where the low original ceiling has been enriched by an Aaltoesque slatted wooden surface, which curves and swirls, defining different areas of activities that curve and swirl below.

Architecturally, the flowing composition carries the eye to loftier and new space beyond, flooded with

natural light through tall walls of glass.

As in most of ZGF's work, artists have been brought in to enhance the architecture, most notably here in Lita Albuquerque's cylindrical, multi-story shaft of light that runs from the roof downward, through floors and ceilings, to the ground floor four levels below.

What ZGF can accomplish starting from scratch in a "state-of-the-art" town library can be seen in the luminous new centerpiece of Bellevue, WA, conceived as a regional "information hub" at the heart of Microsoft heaven. In every sense this is more than a repository for books.

Done by Bob Frasca in company with Seattle partner Evett Ruffcorn, it is one of the most elating buildings that the firm has done.

Rounding the corner like a hand of cards, the eastern and southern elevations are topped by broad, hovering metal roofs, more like great technological awnings than conventional overhangs, and held aloft by constructivist steel struts mounted on circular concrete columns.

Warm light plays beneath the wooden undersides of the projecting roofs, and made warmer still by red sandstone facings below.

The building's radiance can be seen to even better advantage inside, where clerestories pour northern light into an exhilarating three-story space, also lit by windows on the other sides, and organized around an elegant staircase that is a bit grander than one would expect.

But the whole interior is filled with complex yet playful surprises, none more unexpected than the steady processional march of the tall concrete columns through the building. For this is a logical and economic structure

– the same spacing of the colonnade continues in the parking garage below – and its architectonic order, amidst complexity, is a metaphor of the computer age.

Not quite so lyrical, but a happy building nonetheless, the cafeteria for a well-known software company's Redmond West Campus shares some of the mood of the Bellevue Library and even echoes formal elements such as projecting rooflines. Designed two years after the library, it is more of a display of husky Pacific Northwest regionalism. Except for the tall, slender concrete columns, topped by splayed "capitals" that owe more to industrial architecture than to neo-classical tradition, the rest of the building is framed and panelled in reclaimed Douglas fir and composite glu-lam girders and beams. It has an authentic indigenous quality; and ZGF had the chance to create a corporate cafeteria that has the ease and openness of a club.

The idea always is to scale down and open up environments that otherwise would be forbidding. Also at Redmond, for instance, ZGF has master-planned a 46-acre campus for SAFECO. By its very nature the giant insurance company required large office blocks and a data center that could have been massive abstractions. But the humanist planners and architects have scaled them down to something as intelligible as a college campus, once more using a cafeteria as a social center, fronted by a pool.

Whether or not ZGF can always achieve human scale as it tackles larger and larger projects, it will not be for want of trying. A singular test of the firm's philosophy has been met in its proposal for the Mark O. Hatfield Clinical Research Center at the National Institutes of Health in Bethesda, MD. The design won an international competition, as much for the personal consideration given to patients and staff as for the overall concept of a huge health facility where human interaction is to be encouraged and walking distances kept short.

Certainly ZGF's low and midsized brick-faced buildings will be a decisive improvement over its hulking neighbors in the Bethesda complex that, considered as architecture alone, may be fairly described as bureaucratic hives. Landscaped courts, scaled for humans, will relieve the sheer size of the new hospital and labs.

A spectacular glass-walled atrium, where paired staircases will spiral upward like monumental sculpture beneath a handsome skylight, will be a new entrance giving focus and coherence to the entire group of buildings and spaces.

In some ways the Hatfield Center will be to hospital architecture what Eero Saarinen's Dulles International Airport in Washington, D.C., in its original state, was to the architecture of air travel. Little wonder, for ZGF is presently engaged in remaking Portland International Airport (at least so far as arrival and departure access areas are concerned) into a global jetport for the next century.

In earlier work for the airport, where several different firms have been involved, ZGF was partly thwarted by an erratic construction program – more precisely, a non-program of piecemeal changes – which finally is being corrected in a series of bold strokes. Everything from new parking structures and widened approach roads to first-class elevators and escalators, tunnels and cable-stayed pedestrian bridges will be protected from the weather by a single magnificent glass canopy, carried by arching trusses, so that there will be no more slow-ups because of rain.

Eventually the airport will be linked to the superlative MAX light-rail system, on which a ZGF design team, headed by partners Greg Baldwin and Bob Packard, has been working for more than a decade. It is far and away the best urban transit system of its kind in the country, rivaling the finest European models; and perhaps it would be deservedly more famous if it were in a larger American city on the east coast.

As it is, Portland is such a reasonably sized and generally sensible city, saved from sprawl by hills and a river, that a linear rail system makes excellent sense, and is simply regarded as another amenity in an already gracious place. Thus Baldwin's accomplishments probably have not received the praise they warrant.

But no other U.S. architect since Harry Weese did the Washington, D.C., Metro has matched Baldwin's understanding of the aesthetic interrelationship between transportation design and regional growth. Each station has been conceived for a specific site, imparting a distinct local cachet to its architecture and appurtenances, encompassing a public art, landscaping, bus turn-ins, paving materials, even archeological finds uncovered in tunneling, and of course the rational good looks of the German-made light rail vehicles which Baldwin and his team helped to design.

This respect for the past, sensitivity to current needs, and vision of a limitless future add up to a prescription for truly renewing cities.

Without ostentation or flaunting of fads, ZGF as it has grown has solved prototypical problems of technological civilization. By choice, the firm has not yet worked abroad, but takes on such a wide variety of work at home that almost every type of American building, except for private residences (but not multiple dwellings) has been on the boards at one time or another.

Part of the success of its downtown towers in Portland and Seattle, or even of the travertine-clad Federal Building and U.S. Courthouse in Santa Ana which has dignified nethermost Orange County, may be found in ZGF's willingness to follow the urban grain, curving where need be in response to the cityscape. At the University of California in Santa Barbara, on a degraded edge of the campus, the Humanities and Social Sciences Building bends in reply to a now vanished line of trees.

Summing up the whole urban adventure, with both universal and local significance, the California Science Center in south-central Los Angeles, close to the scene of ferocious rioting after the beating of Rodney King, must be counted as one of ZGF's triumphs.

Virtually every conceivable obstacle to civic harmony and progress was overcome in the searching design of the science museum which in many ways is unprecedented. Education, which Diderot said was the first need of the people after bread, has been served by architecture that teaches children (and of course adults) from an infinite range of backgrounds, non-white and white, from the moment they arrive at the entrance plaza. They

learn scientific principles that everyone should know, about the cosmos or planet earth, in fact about everything, as soon as they experience the art of Chuck Hoberman and Larry Kirkland, which teaches them painlessly. No one flunks at the Science Center because the art and architecture, like the exhibits, are meant to be pure joy. As in a cathedral, one sees what one brings; and any troubled kid can smile pedalling a bicycle on a tight rope, which cannot tip as it crosses a thrilling void.

But there is also a powerful historical and architectural lesson to be enjoyed here. The finest spaces are exalting to young and old; and the exterior is a stirring example of contextual design. ZGF, fitting the large museum into a group of older buildings, also saved a neo-classical facade of the former science museum, in brick and terra cotta, which in turn inspired the bi-colored brickwork on the new exteriors. The once famous adjacent rose garden, fallen on evil times, is being brought back to life according to a master plan by ZGF that includes the borders of the USC campus.

Over a million visitors have come to the Science Center since it opened last Christmas; and its popularity has been likened, understandably, to the equal attraction – or more than equal – of the Getty Center miles away on its acropolis in wealthy Brentwood.

The Science Center, by contrast is in the flats. Its architecture lacks the astringent purity of Richard Meier's aristocratical Getty.

Yet that is all to the good. In Athens the Acropolis looked down at the Agora, the forum of everyday life, which nevertheless had its own

temples and altars, courts of laws and democratic assembly halls. It too was sacred to the Gods, especially ingenious Hephaestus, the supreme artificer, revered by all who make things and wish to know their meanings. Today that would include, I'd say, all of Science, wedded in Art, in the work of Zimmer Gunsul Frasca.

Works

Bellevue Regional Library
Bellevue, Washington, 1993

Bellevue is a satellite city of Seattle, separated from it by Lake Washington, but directly connected to Seattle's downtown by thruways and two bridges. The Bellevue Regional Library serves as a catalyst for the growth of a more urbanized community.

Bellevue's growing central business district consists for the most part of 600-foot-long super blocks. Local planners have begun an aggressive long range plan to transform what had been a suburb into a city with a vital urban center. A centerpiece in the implementation of this vision is a central library and future community center at the edge of downtown.

The new state-of the art library and "information hub" for the King County Library System includes the largest reference collection in the 36-library system, public meeting rooms, a 10,000-square-foot children's area, rest rooms and gift shop. Stacks have a capacity of 250,000 volumes. Below-grade parking for 115 cars is included as well as on-site landscaped parking for 80 automobiles.

The new building focuses on a new urban park/plaza that connects to the commercial district by a major pedestrian pathway.

Although the building's geometries are complex and its forms unconventional, the structural system is simple and economical. The structure is patterned on conventional shopping center construction, a fact that made it easy for the builder to bid and construct the design — despite the unusual shapes and angles.

The architects extended the underground parking-lot module's concrete columns upward to support three floors of stacks. By creating an economical structural system, a larger percentage of the budget was dedicated to more visible elements, such as a terne-coated stainless steel roof, wood-faced ceilings and exterior overhangs, and sandstone facades on the south and east sides of the building. Patterned brick veneers were used on the less publicly oriented north and west.

The fragmented south facade of exposed ribbed-concrete columns with an infill of red sandstone opens to a public park and provides an arcade that connects the library to the future community center. A shed-like overhang along the east facade helps diminish the scale of the building so that it harmonizes with the nearby residential neighborhood. Varied roof lines, facade profiles, and fenestration systems further break down the building's apparent size, clarifying its major spaces and functions.

The building interior emphasizes openness and clarity. One of the architects' primary goals was to flood the library with natural light.

The roof's north-facing skylights, clerestories at the juncture of the wall and overhang, and large windows on the first and second floors create bright and cheerful spaces, protected from glare by wood screens and overhangs.

A number of works by Northwest artists — such as glass light fixtures, tiles and cast glass windows — are integrated into the interiors.

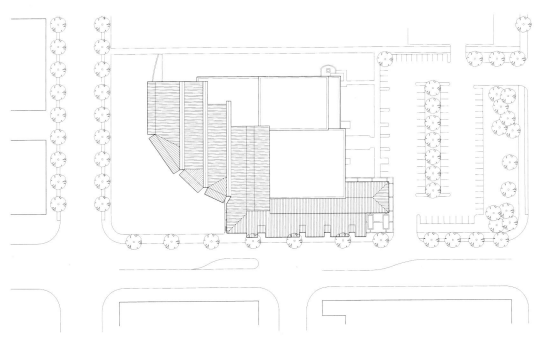

The plan of the library
responds to the
differing circumstances
surrounding the site.
The exterior wall
conditions natural light
differently depending
on the orientation.

Below, differing functions within the library resulted in diverse forms and materials that define them.

Right, first floor,
Second floor,
Upper mezzanine plans.

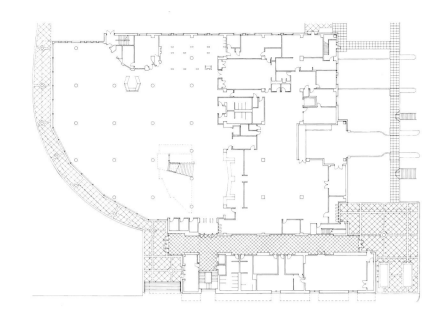

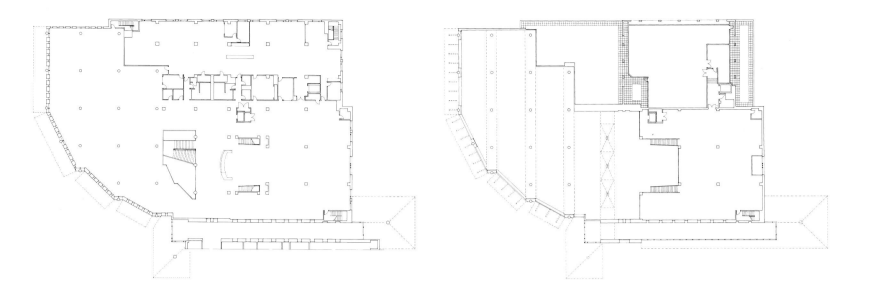

Far left, the public gallery collects patrons from the two principal entrances and directs them to one secure point into the library. Above, natural light is the most important ingredient to the interior.

Below, an open staircase connects the first and second floor reading/stack areas.

The entrance is marked by a giant porch to give it emphasis and serve as the waiting/pick-up area. Transparency is maintained to both expose the activity within and enliven the streetscape.

Peninsula Center Library
Palos Verdes Peninsula, Rolling Hills Estates, California, 1995

Palos Verdes is a beautiful suburban community in the Los Angeles metropolitan area. The existing Peninsula Center Library was a 36,000-square-foot building, completed in 1967 and planned to meet the community's needs for 20 years; however, the community outgrew the building in less than 10. The existing building was no longer in compliance with seismic, energy, or health and safety codes and regulations. The library — which remained operational throughout the phased construction — needed to double its space requirements, as more than half of all reading areas had been replaced by stacks, compact discs, books on cassette, CD-ROM microcomputer workstations, and on-line catalogs.

The architects were asked to design a major addition to the main library, originally designed by Quincy Jones in the 1960s. The existing concrete-frame building is on a steeply sloping site between two arterial streets and comprises three levels: a main library sandwiched between an upper rooftop parking level and a partially underground parking level. The program required that the building size be doubled.

The design solution maintains the existing entrance at the upper street, which continues to be served by the rooftop parking, and adds a new entrance on the lower street 40 feet below. In order to reconcile the condition of four entrances at two levels, a curved wall slices through all levels and acts as the principal orienting device for the entire building.

The yellow wall also separates the public entrance galleries and conference facilities from the controlled access zone of the library itself.

Because the existing building dictated a relatively low ceiling height, the architects provided visual depth to the space by suspending a wood trellis below the ceiling. Circular lights above the trellis give the illusion of skylights.

The building covers most of the site and the mass is relieved by layers of a large-scale trellis, which is horizontal on the upper level and vertical on the lower. The street facades are composed as a series of layered scrims made up of perforated blinds, patterned glass, landscape, and trellis, which filter light and maintain privacy for the reading areas adjacent to the street, while allowing visibility to the activities within. Concrete shear walls tie together existing and new structures, while maintaining visual continuity between the two in a seamless fashion.

A competitive art program resulted in a collaboration of artist and architect that was integral to the building design. Los Angeles-based artists, Lita Albuquerque and Gwynne Murrill, each produced sculptures that are inextricable from their place in the building. Albuquerque's Stellar Axis penetrates all four levels of the library's public entrance galleries, while Murrill's bronze cheetahs and stone column carved with endangered animals, create an atmosphere that is welcoming and enlivening for children.

Plans, from top to
bottom, Roof level,
Third level, Second
level, First level.

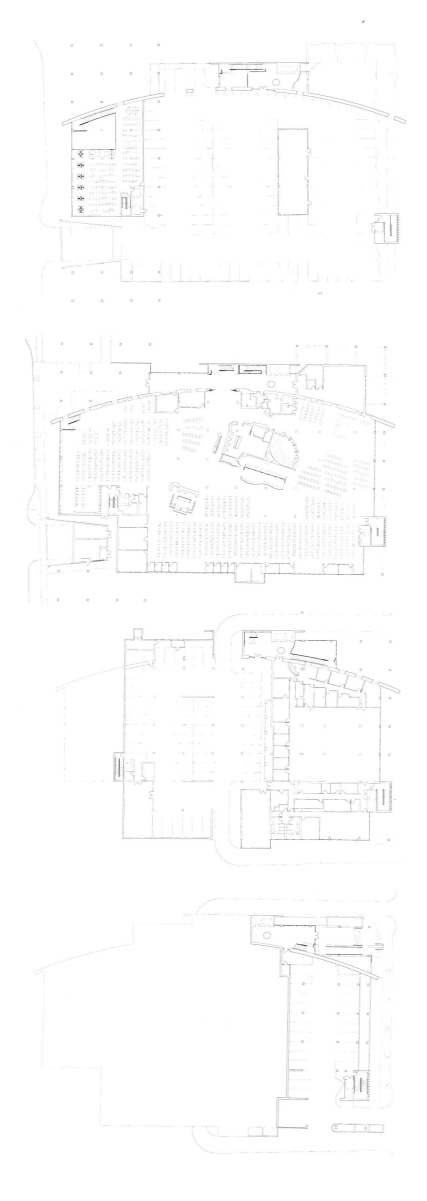

The existing 1960s library was doubled in size and wrapped entirely with a new facade.

A three-foot-thick curved wall separates a four-story zone of public entrance galleries and meeting rooms from the library area.

The facades are
composed of a series
of layers: the outermost
is a space frame that
parallels the street.
Between the space
frame and curtain wall,
trees soften the facade
and filter the California
sun.

Left, artist Gwynne Murrill's bronze cheetah sculpture commands the Young Readers area. Below, the main library floor is organized in a townscape where the service desks, artwork and color accent walls serve as landmarks to visually orient the patron.

Upper right, *Stellar Axis*, an installation created by artist Lita Albuquerque, penetrates all levels of the library's public entrance galleries. Etched-glass doors to the multipurpose room form a separate element in the installation. Lower left, a carved stone column with endangered African animals was designed by artist Gwynne Murrill for the children's area.

Below, the curved wall emerges from the rooftop parking deck to enclose a new lobby on the building's fourth floor. Right, the new pedestrian entrance on the lower street 40 feet below.

High Technology Corporate Campus Cafeteria
Redmond, Washington, 1995

The objective was to design a 30,000-square-foot cafeteria, seating 750, to serve as the focal point of a new 725,000-square-foot campus for a high technology corporation. The campus is comprised of five office buildings, parking for 2,800 cars, extensive site development, and central plant, in addition to the cafeteria.

The campus is a pedestrian-oriented arrangement of buildings that reflect a high quality work environment consistent with the culture of this world renowned software company. The campus is organized around a central landscaped courtyard to create a collegial atmosphere and to encourage employee interaction. Located in the center of the campus, the cafeteria is intended to be the focal point for this creative exchange of ideas. The unusual building was conceived to be in stark contrast to the prescribed work environment of the office buildings and designed to have the relaxed and casual atmosphere of a mountain lodge.

The lofty dining rooms take full advantage of the site by opening up to the morning sun, views east to the Cascade mountain range, and to the central courtyard.

The cafeteria is a two-story volume containing two separate dining environments. Each level of the cafeteria can be accessed separately from the exterior. The main floor features the primary lobby, and seats 500 people, served by a standard style servery. Continuous sliding glass doors allow the dining room to spill out to the exterior terrace adjacent to the lake and stream. The upper level, which seats 250 people, is designed as a Bistro/deli. It adjoins a terrace and sports courts.

The informal appearance of the building is reinforced by utilizing heavy sandblasted cast-in-place concrete walls and columns juxtaposed with an exposed wood roof structure. The simple interior of the dining rooms is filled with natural light from large clerestory windows and is visually warmed by the natural light reflecting off the wood paneling, stair railings and roof decking. All of the wood used in the building, except for the glu-lam beams, is milled from reclaimed Douglas Fir.

Located in the center
of campus, the cafeteria
is the focal point and
a casual retreat from
the prescribed work
environment of the
surrounding office
buildings.

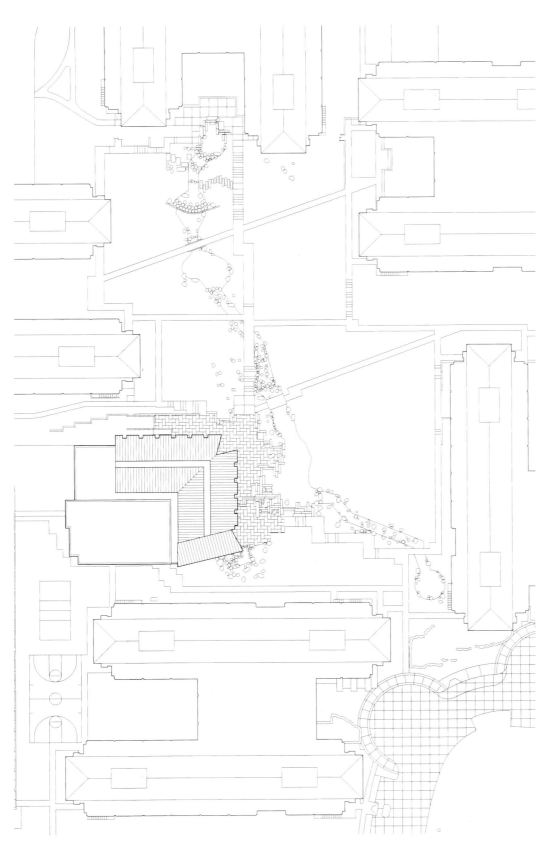

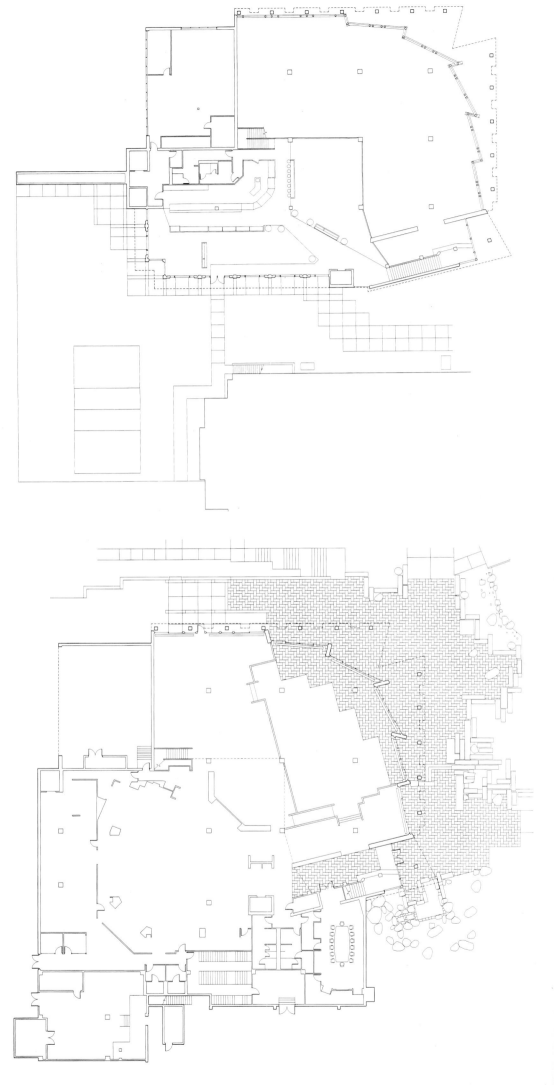

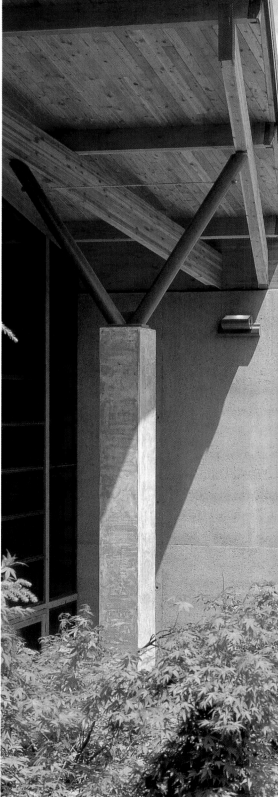

The large volume dining spaces capitalize on views to the adjacent courtyard and outside terrace, and the mountains beyond.

The interior dining spaces are filled with natural light from floor-to-ceiling sliding glass doors and clerestory windows. Sandblasted concrete walls and columns are warmed by an exposed wood roof structure and wood paneling.

Humanities and Social Sciences Building, University of California,
Santa Barbara, California, 1996

With its Mediterranean climate and Pacific coastal location, the UC Santa Barbara campus is one of the most beautiful in the country. For much of its short history though the campus grew without the benefit of a master plan. By the 1980's, a plan that described the pattern of pathways and open spaces was imposed to bring about orderly future development.

To strengthen and unify the campus, the Humanities and Social Sciences Building was sited on a former parking lot in a previously undefined area of campus.

The new 153,672-square-foot building is designed to play a dual role in the community life of the campus. Located on a triangular site, the design serves the school's academic program in a manner that gives equal priority to strengthening the environment of the campus at large.

The east boundary of the site is the curved Arts Lane which is the pedestrian extension of the entrance to the University, while the southern boundary is a pedestrian corridor traversed by more than 16,000 students daily on foot and on bicycles. Finally, two important view and access corridors link the site with the natural park surrounding the Lagoon south of the campus. The building houses a diverse set of university programs in the departments of Anthropology, Asian-American Studies, Classics, Drama and Dance, History, Philosophy, and Religious Studies.

The program components are organized into four connected academic elements; a one-story wing for drama and dance; two four-story elements for classroom space and academic offices; and at the prominent northeast corner of the site, a six-story academic and administrative office block. The block, by means of its height, complex roof profile, and pinnacle open-stair tower, provides an anchor and definition for the building.

The wings form a landscaped quadrangle that will channel cross-campus pedestrian circulation toward a major campus east-west corridor.

The quadrangle, just as importantly, creates a much needed sense of place for the entire campus community.

Three front doors address the surroundings with equal clarity and the two edges of the complex define major campus bikeways. The arcades and porches both direct pedestrian flow and punctuate activity centers at several points at the edges of the complex.

The building, which uses traditional Santa Barbara materials, is a predominantly stucco exterior. The building base, including the window and door surrounds, is of a rusticated precast concrete.

The site was a parking lot in a precinct of the campus which lacked clear definition and a sense of place. The varied series of roof forms explain the diversity of the interrelated disciplines housed within.

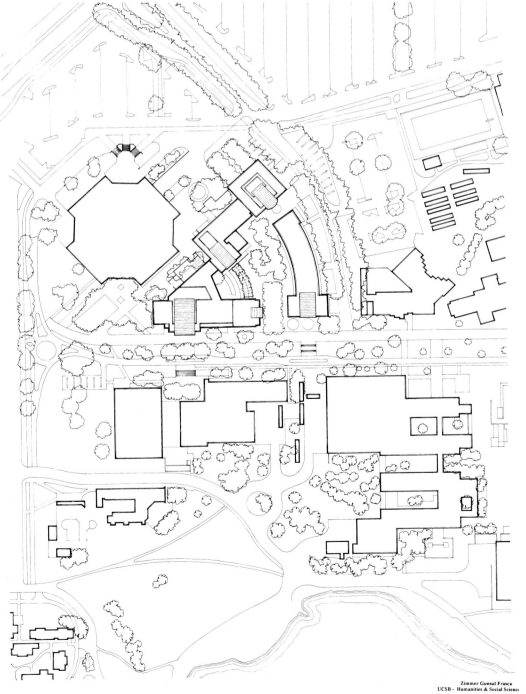

Zimmer Gunsul Frasca
UCSB - Humanities & Social Science

The top floor is defined by double the normal window area, and a sandstone, slate and limestone tile frieze. The building is capped by an overhang with articulated ribs and a stainless steel roof edge.

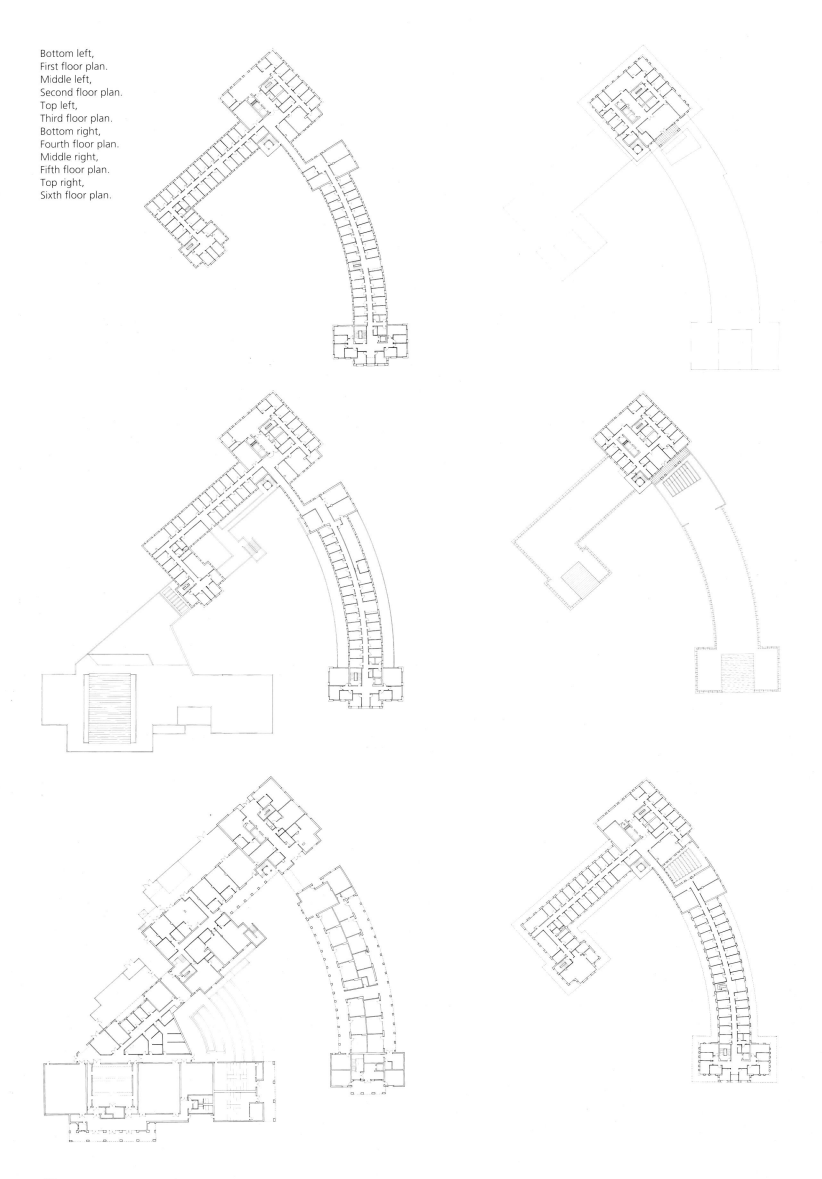

Bottom left,
First floor plan.
Middle left,
Second floor plan.
Top left,
Third floor plan.
Bottom right,
Fourth floor plan.
Middle right,
Fifth floor plan.
Top right,
Sixth floor plan.

The building provides classrooms, dance and drama studios, research space, offices and colloquium facilities.

Reed College
Gray Campus Center
Portland, Oregon, 1997

By the early 1990s, the majority of social functions on the Reed College campus were served by two facilities: a 40,600-square-foot two building Commons complex and a 12,000-square-foot Student Union building.

Inefficiencies in these facilities combined with the college's desire to improve student life prompted Reed to consider building a new Campus Center. The program contains all of the functions housed in the existing Commons and Student Union facilities and adds a multipurpose Auditorium for films, lectures, banquets, and music performances. In addition to addressing these functional criteria, the college wanted to tie the new facility into the current Tudor Gothic architectural vocabulary of the campus. The new Campus Center would respect the existing quadrangle of which it would become a part and invigorate the campus as the heart of student activity.

The new 73,000-square-foot Gray Campus Center includes three integrated components: a 42,000-square-foot renovated Commons, a 12,000-square-foot remodeled Student Union, and a new 19,000-square-foot multipurpose Auditorium. Tying the three components together is a covered brick arcade which wraps the Commons on two sides and connects to both the Student Union and the Auditorium. This new arcade respects the materials of other campus facilities in the use of brick, including the Old Dorm Block opposite the new Campus Center.

The main component of the Campus Center, the two-story Commons, includes the main dining hall, kitchen and servery; a cafe; student organization offices; student activity spaces; the college bookstore; and a post office. The previously separated two-building complex is now joined as a single unit with a defining peaked entry and skylit atrium. Renovation of the Commons focused on improving the coordination between the lower-level kitchen and the main-level dining hall.

The key to the solution is in relocating the kitchen to the main level, in proximity to the dining hall, and adding a multistation servery between the two. The large dining hall is subdivided by low partitions which create cozy eating nooks while maintaining the overall function of the large hall.

While many of the functions housed in the new Commons existed in the original building, the facility now also features a new cafe along its southern side to provide an inviting social area for students.

Sited on the east side of the Commons and connected by the brick arcade is the Student Union.

The third and final component of the new Campus Center, the Auditorium, defines a new western edge of the Commons Quad and completes the fourth side of the quadrangle. The Auditorium, like the Union, is linked to the Commons by the covered brick arcade.

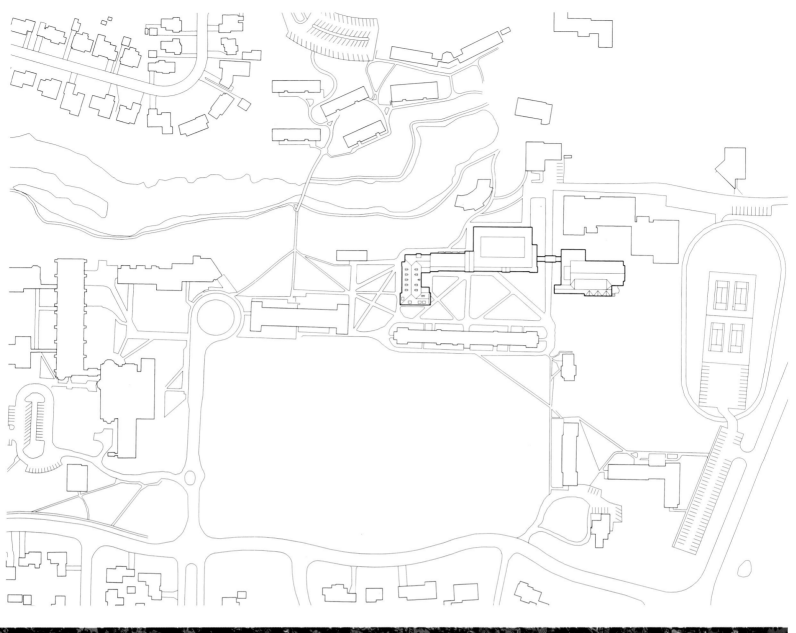

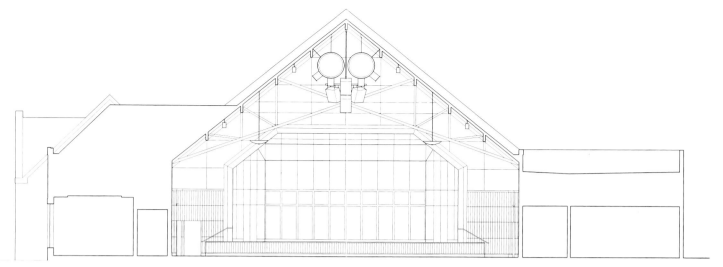

With the remodel of the Student Union and the addition of the Auditorium, the existing architectural vocabulary was changed to relate to the traditional brick buildings on the opposite side of the quad. An arcade was added to connect the expanded Campus Center, to provide an outdoor extension of the dining hall as a gathering place for students, and exterior circulation in inclement weather.
Upper left, Site plan; Upper right, Section through Auditorium.

Above, the existing dining hall was infused with natural light by inserting dormers into the roof and replacing solid portions of the north wall with floor-to-ceiling windows. The interior space is divided with low partitions to create more intimate seating areas, while maintaining views.

Right, the Auditorium is designed primarily for music but has the ability to serve as multi-purpose space for dance, lectures, etc. Moveable seating and bleachers can be arranged in a number of configurations. Below, Upper level and Lower level plans.

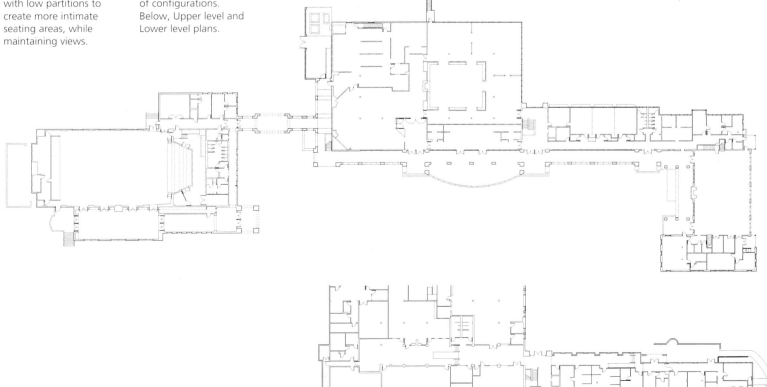

Below and right, the north side of the building was reclad in stucco, chosen because it could be supported on the existing wood frame structure, and provide a lighter facade facing the canyon. Left, brick was utilized on the south side to relate to the existing quad.

William R. Wiley Environmental Molecular Sciences Laboratory
Richland, Washington, 1997

The 204,665-gross-square-foot Environmental Molecular Sciences Laboratory (EMSL) is the US Department of Energy's newest national scientific user facility.

The mission of the EMSL is to develop new knowledge and technologies that will reduce the cost and increase the effectiveness of environmental restoration and waste management efforts undertaken on DOE sites. The facility is intended to enhance education and training experiences, and to encourage collaboration and technology transfer among federal agencies, state and local governments, industry, and academia world-wide.

Given that visiting scientists from all over the world are brought to this relatively remote setting, the need to create an environment conducive to interaction was a primary design goal.

On the research side, it was determined that the sophisticated equipment and intensive laser use (plus unknown future equipment, 2-3 times more advanced than what currently exists) required highly technical and flexible space that would be best accommodated by large, windowless volumes. It was also important that personnel access to labs did not interfere with movement of equipment and materials. Offices for scientists were not to be housed in the labs, given DOE and life safety code requirements. These issues provided the key drivers for the concept and organization of the building design.

The primary building blocks of laboratories, offices, and the seminar/administrative functions are connected horizontally by a circulation system of two primary corridors – a main spine for movement of people,

and a secondary spine for transport of equipment. The laboratories, computer facility, and lab support areas are housed in a one-story structure comprising about 85,000 square feet. Locating the laboratories on one floor, at grade, provides vibration isolation for all experimental lab clusters and flexibility for expansion. Running along the western edge of the lab component is the secondary corridor, providing unrestricted access between the labs and the loading dock, large service yards, machine shop, and other maintenance areas. A series of service corridors intersect with this corridor, providing distribution of building and laboratory systems, delivery of equipment and supplies directly to the labs.

Exterior design and massing of the building is intended to break down the scale of the primarily one-story complex. The articulation of the office pods creates a village-like primary facade. Brick was chosen as the primary exterior material to help counter the remote nature of the site by creating a collegiate campus identity for the new complex. A deep red brick is accented by white steel columns.

Below, offices for scientific staff are housed in three two-story structures forming the primary facade. An effort was made to take advantage of the outdoors, with both visual and physical connections, for all of the non-laboratory spaces.
Right, Site plan.

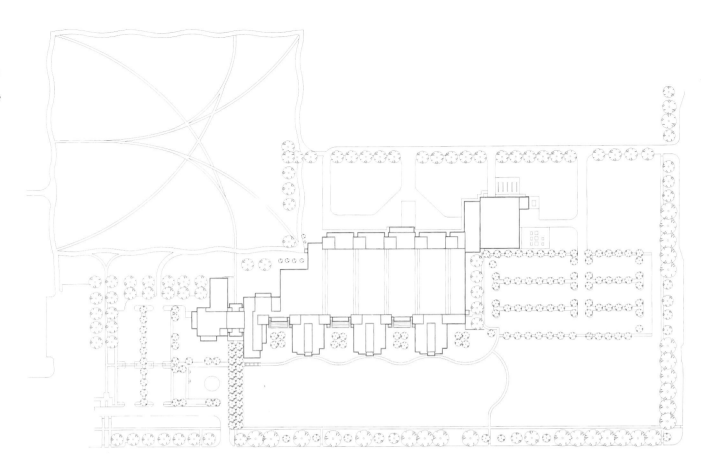

Left, brick serves
as the primary building
material in an effort
to create a collegiate
campus identity in this
remote setting.

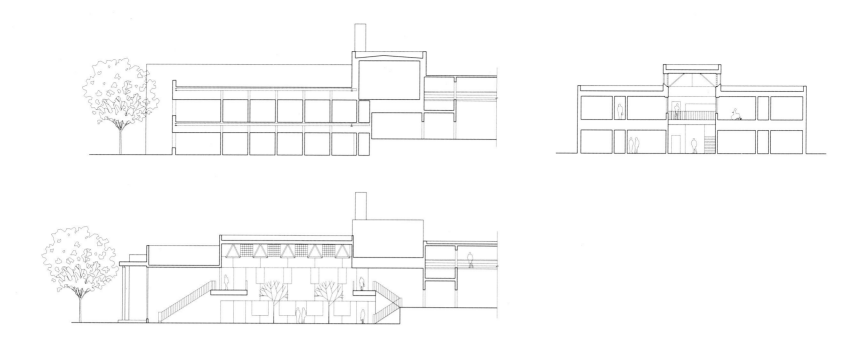

Above, East-West and
North-South sections.
Below, First floor and
Second floor/Office
level plans.

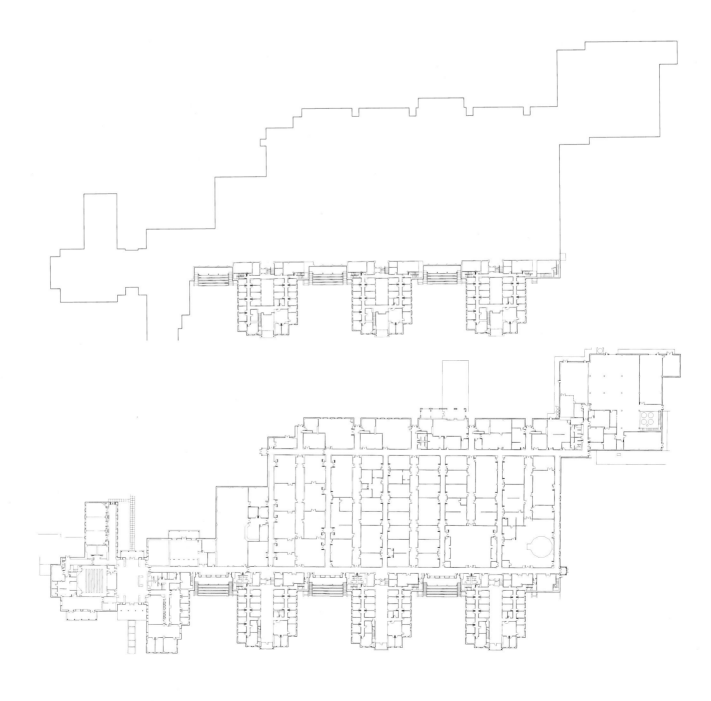

Offices are arranged
around a two-story
atrium space that serves
as a lounge for informal
gatherings. From the
main lobby, above left,
access is provided to the
administration/seminar
area, which includes
a small dining room,
lower right.

California Science Center
Los Angeles, California, 1998

The California Science Center occupies a prominent site at the heart of the 160-acre Exposition Park, at the southwest edge of downtown Los Angeles.

In 1990 two of the museum's historic buildings were closed for earthquake safety reasons, precipitating the current new building project. The first stage of the work resulted in a master plan for Exposition Park prepared by ZGF.

The plan proposed that the museum (previously housed in eight separate structures) consolidate its facilities under one roof on a site directly south of the seven-acre sunken Rose Garden, centerpiece in arguably the most intact grouping of historic civic buildings in Los Angeles. By 1992, the Master Plan implementation began with the renovation and expansion of the museum into a state-of-the-art learning facility.

The new 245,000-square-foot building includes interactive exhibits; a Science Court, a 3-D IMAX Theater, conference center, seminar/board room, special exhibits gallery, food and retail services.

The new science center is arranged into five major elements: a freestanding theater (rotated 45 degrees from the main building to follow the existing road alignment); a semi-enclosed rotunda (connecting theater and museum); the main exhibition block of the science center (bisected by an 80-foot-high wedge of skylit space); the 300-foot-long second level Science Court; and finally, the restored north wing of the original building. Visitors enter the rotunda and proceed directly to either museum or theater. The building's ground level houses the museum store, public meeting rooms and restaurants, and opens up to the wedge-shaped skylit space, through which one ascends to the cross-axial Science Court overlooking restaurants and the Rose Garden.

The dramatic Science Court atrium and outer Science Plaza feature a series of art experiences which demonstrate scientific principles, such as artist Chuck Hoberman's kinetic unfolding *Hypar*, or solar display utilizing light refraction and color by artist Larry Kirkland.

The composition of the building places the black box of exhibition spaces behind the glazed "galleria" of the Science Court. This serves as a backdrop for the historic facade clad in dark red brick and beige terra cotta. The gently-curved south facade and the theater are clad in geometric tile patterns. A curtain of perforated stainless steel backs the rotunda and is repeated at all ground level entrances.

Exposition Park Master
Plan, with aerial view of
the new California
Science Center looking
north.

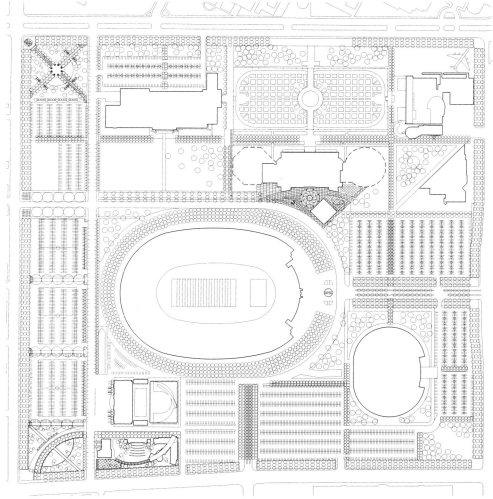

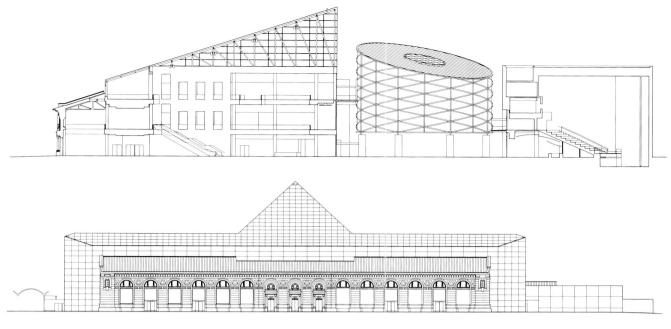

The shape of the building responds to the symmetry of the Rose Garden on the north and the alignment of the existing Coliseum promenade on the south. Left, North/South section; North elevation.

The north wing of the 1913 Howard F. Ahmanson Building was incorporated into the new structure. The center of the historic facade was rebuilt with salvaged brick and integrated into the new building, which restored the north perimeter of the landmark Rose Garden.

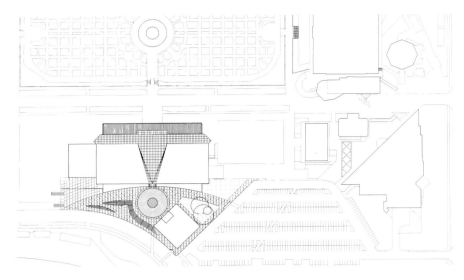

The three-story open-air rotunda serves as a collection space, where visitors gather before entering the museum. Ramps attached to the inside of the rotunda provide upper-floor connections between the IMAX theater and the exhibition spaces of the main building.

Below, *Aerial*, designed
by artist Larry Kirkland,
consists of some 1,600
gold- and palladium-
leaf spheres suspended
from the ceiling with a
granite bench depicting
a cross section of a
DNA strand underneath
them.
Below, First floor and
Second floor plan.

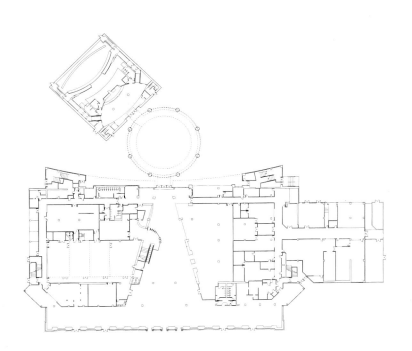

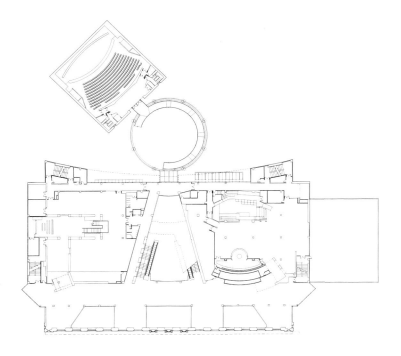

The steel exoskeleton of the central rotunda is clad in panels of perforated stainless steel. A skylight of dichroic glass casts color reflections on the ground, the tile walls, and on the *Aerial* installation.

Inside, the open lobby of the Science Court gives way on upper floors to loft-like spaces for the various exhibits. Chuck Hoberman's kinetic sculpture, *Hypar*, is suspended 42 feet above visitors, and expands from 15 feet to 50 feet.

Exhibit design includes
permanent installations
gathered in two
thematic environments,
The World of Life and
the Creative World.
Subject matter ranges
from the atom to the
cosmos to computer
technology.

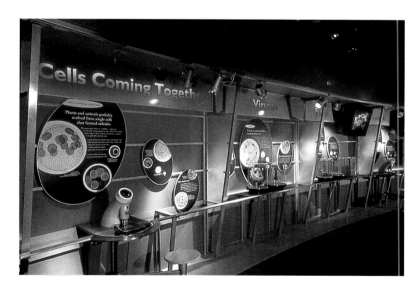

Doernbecher Children's Hospital
Portland, Oregon, 1998

The new 80-bed, 250,000-square-foot Doernbecher Children's Hospital is a multifaceted project which seeks to meet not only its own requirements, but also recognize diverse site, campus planning and critical programmatic relationships on the Oregon Health Sciences University campus.

No feasible conventional site existed, so one had to be created. Spanning the canyon that separates the north and south sections of the Oregon Health Sciences University Medical Campus, the new Doernbecher Children's Hospital connects to critical programmatic areas which are integral to the hospital's mission. To the north is University Hospital South with the Doernbecher Children's Hospital Neonatal Intensive Care Unit and critical shared imaging surgery and treatment areas. To the south is the Childhood Development and Rehabilitation Center.

The new hospital is organized on five levels. The entry level, Level 3, at SW Campus Drive, houses reception/admission, the public lobby, gift shop and coffee bar.

The next level up is Level 7 (floors corresponding to University Hospital South), which houses pediatric medical clinics, specialty and surgery clinics, psychiatry/psychology, rehabilitation, imaging and pharmacy.

Level 8 holds critical functions for the new hospital, including a 16-bed Pediatric Intensive Care Unit, new operating and recovery rooms, day hospital functions and cardiac diagnostic areas. This is the first of two levels of the hospital to make direct connections to the University Hospital South.

Level 9 has two 24 single occupancy bed medical/surgery units, one unit dedicated to adolescent and the other to younger children. This floor also has three landscaped courtyards, one dedicated as a child play space, one reserved for staff and the third for patient families. Floor 10 is the Cancer Center, with a 16-bed medical/surgery unit for immune deficient and compromised patients.

A theme of nature and natural processes is manifested throughout the interior. Artists have collaborated throughout this project to enrich the experiences of the patients, visitors and staff. For example, artist Margot Thompson has created silk-screened glass and ceramic frit patterns on patient room windows in themes of tree leaves, seashells, bird and animal tracks. Using typography, calligraphy and printmaking techniques, poet Kim Stafford and artist Margot Thompson have collaborated in the Level 8 waiting areas. Metal sculptor Wayne Chabre has created an inviting central courtyard based on a nature island theme. The primary elements include a copper roof pavilion (adorned with varieties of birds), and a playful tent trimmed with a copper fish.

The bridge-like structure of the new hospital provides important connections to shared services on the medical school campus. The main public entrance to the hospital is at the base of the canyon, adjacent to new and existing parking.
Below, Site plan.

The building's suspended curvilinear exterior consists of a metal panel curtain wall system and glass. Departments are organized along a curved circulation spine, which serves as an orienting device and connects both sides of the canyon with views of Portland.
Below, the center shaft of the building includes the lobby and vertical circulation.

The main lobby is a primary focus of the art program. A 120-foot frieze of cut-out animals and plants, by artists Frank Boyden and Brad Rude, spans the upper section of the windows in a 3-foot, 5-inch band, illustrating the overall theme of nature.

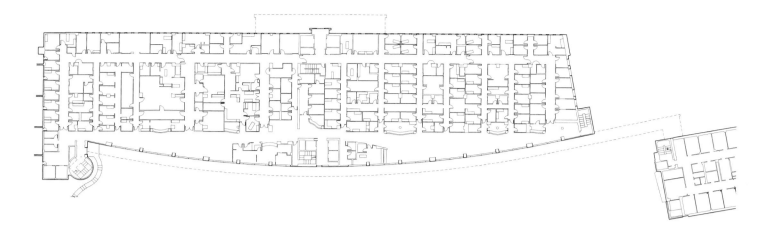

Waiting areas on the
outpatient clinic floor
serve the exam rooms
and contain play
activities for the
patients.
Top, Level 7 and, right,
Level 8 plans.

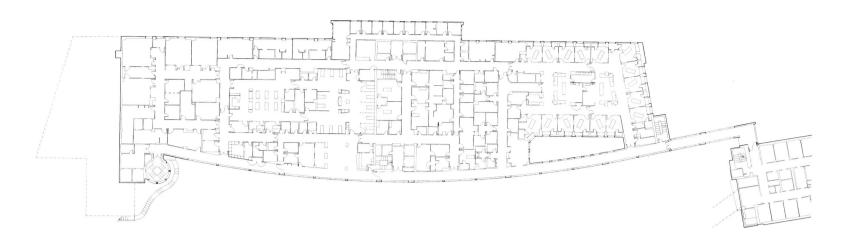

Below, Level 9 and,
right, Level 10 plans.

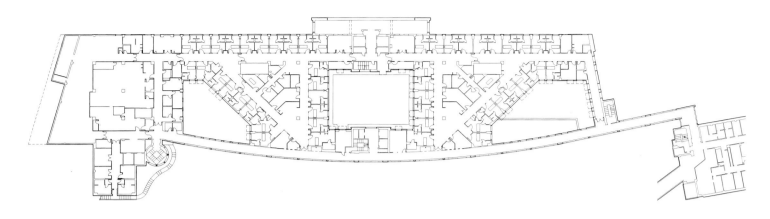

Each patient room looks
out upon one of three
inner courtyards, which
provide outdoor play
areas and visual
connections to the
outside for patients,
along with respite for
staff and families.

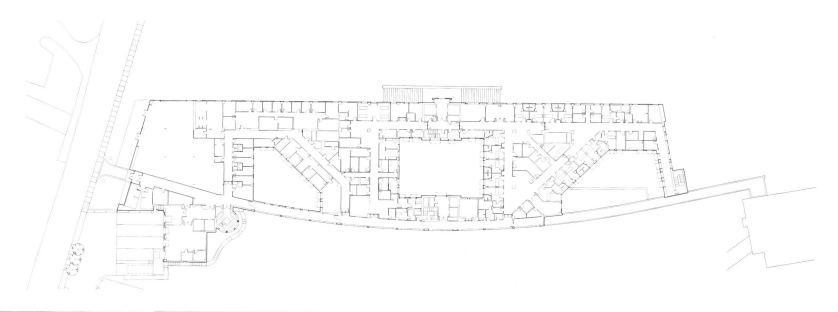

Below, a meditation room on Level 10 is the result of a collaboration with artists Jim Hirschfield and Sonya Ishii.

Westside Light Rail Corridor
Portland, Oregon, 1998

Based on the success of Portland's light rail system MAX, the decision was made to extend the system 15 miles from the downtown, through Portland's West Hills, and into suburban Beaverton and Hillsboro.

The goal is to continue to build a region-wide network of mass transit that improves access, develops the area's economy, revitalizes surrounding communities, and enhances the environment.

The design and operation of the Westside Light Rail Corridor is derived from precedents established by the Banfield Transitway. However, the Westside system also explores new concepts as it responds to different physical, economic and social environments. The Westside will utilize the first high-speed, low-floor, light rail cars in the world. Not only do the cars provide ideal access for those with disabilities, but they also allow the system to fit in existing environments without obtrusive raised platforms.

Artists were employed as part of the architectural team on the project. While the artists have produced some integrated works of art, their principal contribution has been to expand the story transit tells as it visits a succession of neighborhoods and communities. In the process, the transit system functions as both a purveyor of service and a reminder of the heritage and aspirations of those that it serves. While the purpose of the artists' contribution is not novel, their ability to challenge and stretch the symbolic value of the architecture is unique.

As the MAX heads west of the downtown, its first stop is Civic Stadium. The station is set in an open plaza across the street from Portland's only outdoor sports arena. A curved substation building responds to the stadium's curves and arches and provides seating facing the plaza and the trains. Lights in the substation's windows brighten to signal approaching trains. Designated the "communication station," the stop celebrates the importance of communication to the vitality of Portland. An essay on the communication building's steel panels profiles some of the more eccentric contributors to the city's history. Bronze podiums in the plaza – shaped like a stump, a soapbox and a pedestal – invite spontaneous orators; and benches on the platform are shaped like punctuation marks, providing emphasis to speakers' words.

Proceeding from the stadium, the Westside alignment enters a three-mile-long tunnel and stops at the Washington Park Zoo station which, at 260 feet below grade, is the deepest in North America. Four high-speed elevators will carry passengers up to the zoo, which attracts more visitors than any other site in Oregon.

Emerging from the tunnel, the Westside travels toward the system's third major station, Sunset Transit Center. Serving an area that is rapidly becoming a Northwest hub for high-tech research and manufacturing, this station will emphasize technology in its design.

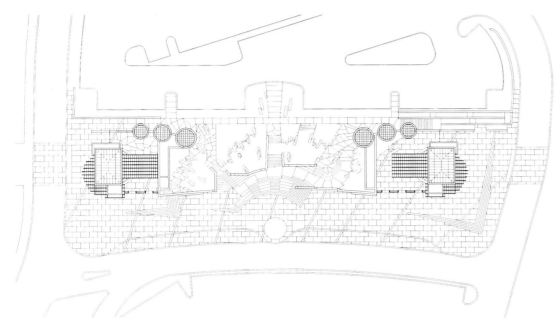

Left, Washington Park Station site plan. Middle left, Looking from the Kiss (of the tunnel boring machine) toward the Blast (of the tunnel excavation) and upper garden of the Washington Park Station; middle right, the surface entrance framed by the tunnel exhaust stacks.

Lower left, the best light rail tunnel station is one good room, shared by vehicle and patron, that introduces the world above.

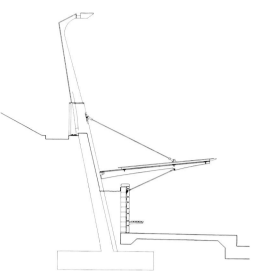

Above, the plaza and elevators linking Sunset Transit Center's bus facilities at the right with the rail station below.
Left, as the elevator shafts and the grass guardrails portray the machine in the garden, they synthesize the technology of the light rail system and the agricultural heritage of the place.

The Stadium Station's traction power stations, signal/com stations and random pedestals, soap boxes and stumps are all transformed and located to accommodate and convey the art of communication.

All surface stations are simple, inviting, durable, and very much a part of the neighborhoods they serve.

Portland International Airport Terminal Access Program
Portland, Oregon, 1999

Portland International Airport (PDX) has been consistently rated as one of the most user-friendly airports in the world. Double-digit passenger increases in recent years also make it one of the fastest growing airports in the United States. In order to address the facility needs caused by such growth, the airport launched the most ambitious development program in its 56-year history. The first component of this development involves the Terminal Access Program (TAP). This program will increase close-in parking and improve terminal access in order to carry the airport into the 21st century.

The goal is to meet the demands of greater traffic while also maintaining the superior facilities and service that travelers through PDX have come to expect.

The existing three-story airport parking garage will expand to seven levels, more than tripling in size from 1,050 public parking spaces to 3,300. The enlarged garage will also bring passengers closer to the airport as five of the seven levels extend toward the terminal building. Pedestrian bridges, expanded tunnels, and an improved baggage claim roadway level will lead travelers to the terminal from the garage.

Access to the airport will greatly improve through the addition of vehicle lanes on both the upper (ticket lobby) and lower (baggage claim) levels of the terminal roadway. Four new lanes will be added to the existing four lanes at the ticket lobby level, with three more lanes added on the lower level as well. These additional lanes will help relieve traffic congestion and, combined with new center islands, provide more curb space for passenger loading and unloading.

Overhead pedestrian bridges will connect the new parking facilities to the terminal, with a 100,000 SF glass canopy covering the entire roadway system. Inside the terminal, the main building's east wall will move 25 feet further east, enlarging both the ticket lobby and baggage claim areas. New elevators, escalators and stairs will also be constructed east of their current locations, improving circulation and enhancing the overall experience for travelers.

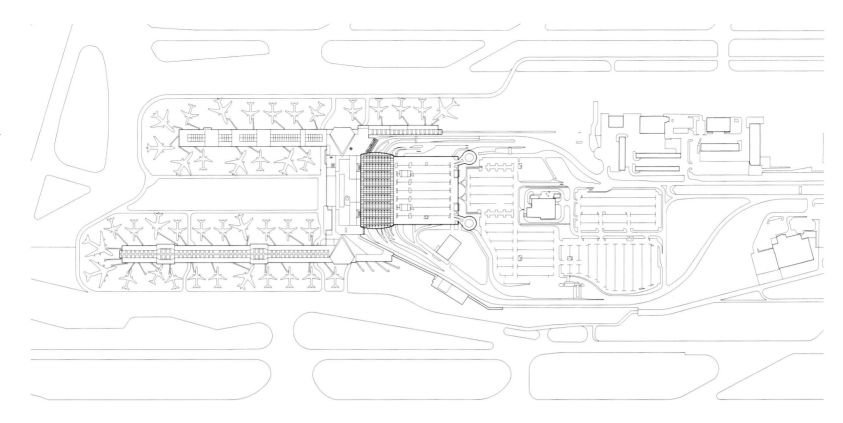

Below, the serpentine
shape of the pedestrian
bridges was driven by
the need to connect the
vertical circulation
systems of the terminal
and the parking garage,
each located at varying
points.

Plans, clockwise,
Enplaning level,
Canopy Roof level,
Bridge level,
Deplaning level.

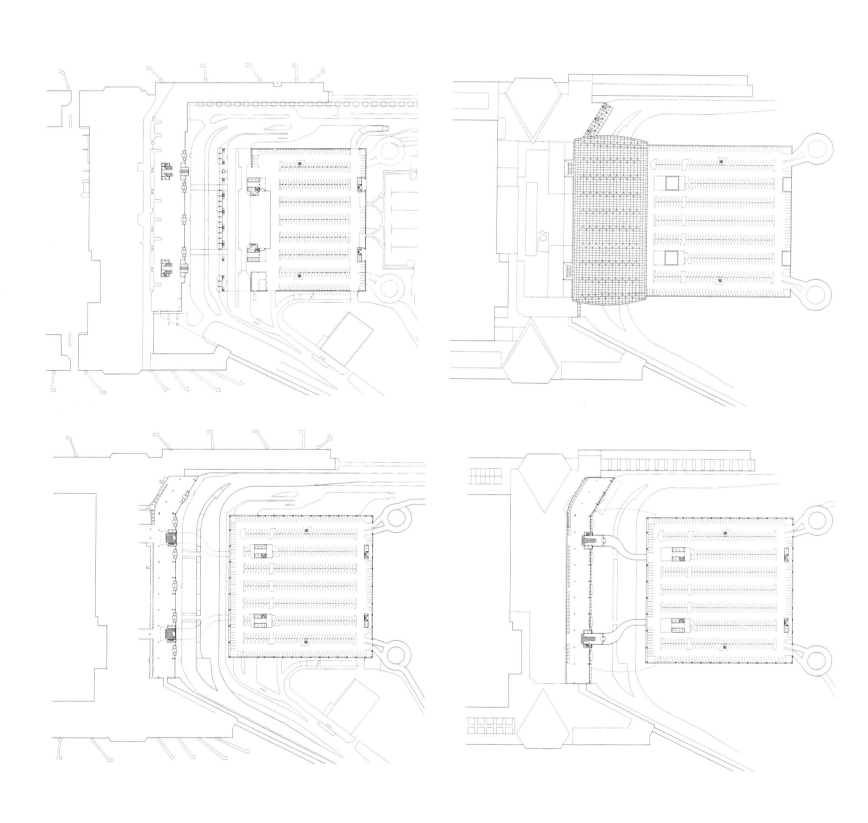

The goal of increasing parking and access to the terminal, while maximizing sheltered curb space, resulted in a grand public room which physically integrates parking with terminal activities.

The structure of the
bridge is suspended
from the roof above.

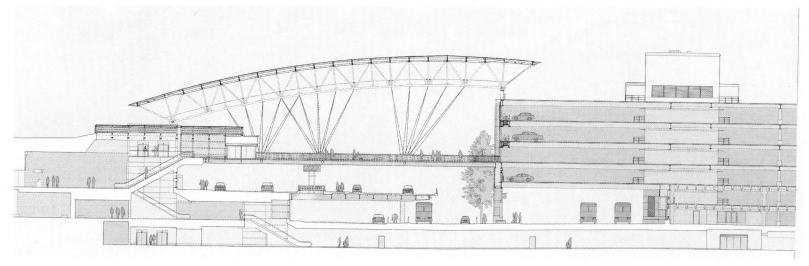

ODS Tower
Portland, Oregon, 1999

The objective was to design an office and retail building at a site at the principal gateway to downtown Portland, Oregon.

The ODS Tower is a 24-story downtown mixed-use development consisting of 356,000 square feet of office, 33,300 square feet of retail, a 5,700-square-foot day care facility, and 400 above-grade parking spaces on six levels.

The architecture is sculptural with facades changing on each side of the building in response to various parts of the city. A gently curved east facade orients to the Willamette River. Other rectilineal facades reinforce the grid of the neighboring streets of the downtown.

The retail and parking components are located in the base structure which will reach 67 feet above the street level. Parking is located on three half-floor levels on the northern half of the site, opposite the two levels of retail on the southern half of the site, which fronts Morrison Street, Portland's 100% retail avenue. There are three full levels of parking above the retail and parking floors.

The office component includes a mid-block, double height entrance lobby at grade facing Second Avenue, and 17 levels of office floors above the six story retail and parking base structure. The office tower floors range from 25,500 square feet at the lower levels, to roughly 22,000 square feet at the mid-height floors and 19,800 square feet at the top levels. The office tower sets back at levels 9, 12, 21, and 24 on the west, south and north facades, creating opportunities for roof terraces.

The proposed materials for the exterior wall consist of a combination of flamed and polished light colored granite and precast, with aluminum and glass store front glazing and curtain wall.

The curve of the east facade and the inset west face of the tower are accented by horizontal window bands and complemented by bands of granite or precast spandrels.

The north, south and west facades of the office tower are punched windows framed in a grid of precast.

A major sculptural installation will span the building's entryway. Inspired by her first trip to Oregon, sculptor Judy Pfaff will create a mixed-media composition focused around a large cedar trunk. The imagery will call attention to the state's majestic trees both in terms of natural beauty and economic vitality. Integrating natural and man-made elements, including tubular steel, the sculpture will further represent the connection between nature and architecture, and between the sculptural elements and the building.

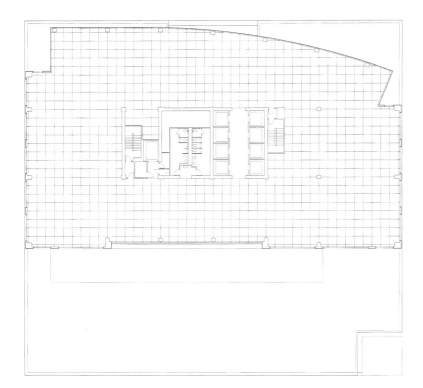
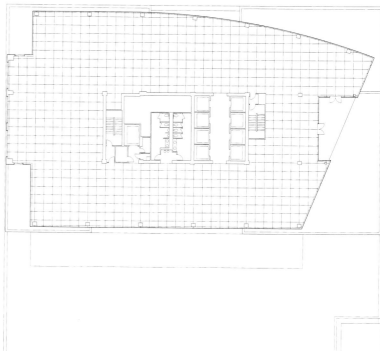

The varied facades
of the office tower
are in response to the
varying urban fabric
surrounding it, coupled
with opportunities
for views. The site in
downtown Portland is
crucial in connecting
the retail core with the
waterfront.
Right, Site plan.
Top, 12th floor plan,
24th floor plan.

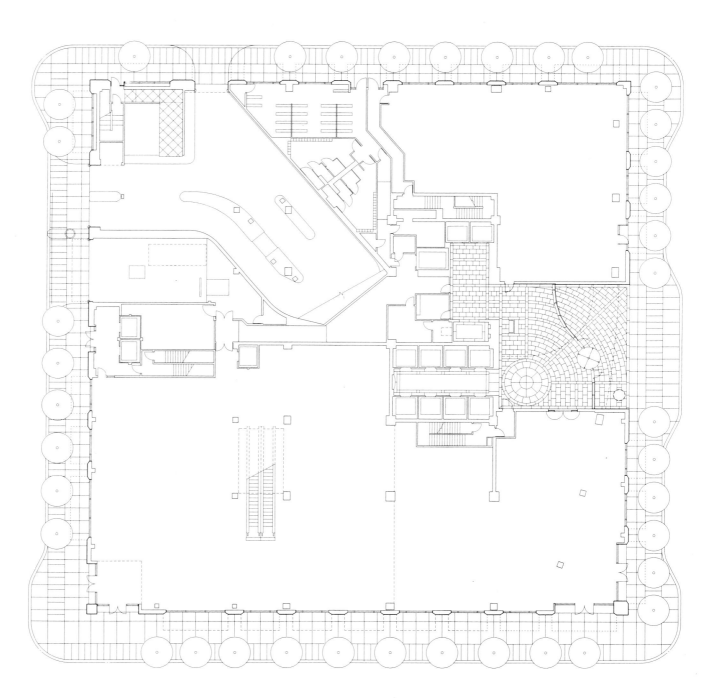

Right, a major public artwork by artist Judy Pfaff, awarded through a national competition, is incorporated into the main lobby, the result of the Regional Arts Commission Percent for Art program.

US Food and Drug Administration
Irvine, California, 2000

This 133,000-square-foot laboratory and office facility for the Los Angeles District of the US Food and Drug Administration represents a marked departure from the norms of both government buildings and contemporary laboratory buildings. It is designed to reflect a profound change in the organization of the laboratory and administrative functions of this regulatory agency— its attempt to reinvent itself from the inside out. Previously, FDA employees specialized in individual segments of work, all located in separate buildings. The new model is found in flexible teams which will perform field, testing, and administrative duties interchangeably, at the same site.

The site is 10-acres at the southwestern edge of the marshy wetlands of upper Newport Bay, located across a protected natural habitat from the University of California campus, with uninterrupted views of the Saddleback mountains to the northeast. Three boxy two-story laboratory blocks are arranged in an open semi-circle on high ground at the very margin of the wetland. They will be constructed of cast-in-place concrete left in its natural state to form the south and west-facing back wall of the building. Openings in these walls are limited, but carefully placed to afford natural light and views from every aisle in the laboratories.

Hung directly upon these sturdy laboratory blocks (and dependent upon them for lateral stability) are two lightweight steel-framed office trays facing northeast to the wetland and mountain views. The spatial continuum from laboratory bays through a glass wall into open-plan offices and to the sweeping vista is uninterrupted and staff teams can observe and interact with each other openly. Opposite the laboratory blocks the two office levels are enclosed by a sloped curtain of glass set back to open up a vertical cavity of space between the two floors. Open stairs located at the edge of the upper level facilitate movement and interaction between staff teams on both levels.

The scale and sweep of the two-story glass wall on the exterior plays to the views back toward the building from the nearest public roadway more than a quarter-mile across the wetland. By day it will reflect the sky and by night it will reveal the industry of the building's occupants. This continuous wall is the backdrop for a series of events which mark the functions of the building, beginning with the yawning vortex of the public entrance at its head, punctuated by the concrete emplacement of the dining and administrative block, and completed by the circular hermetic tower of the library and computer training center at its tail. Finally a family of curved, corrugated copper screen walls envelops the conference center, the exit stairs, and the mechanical penthouses, crawling up and over and contrasting with the concrete hardness of the earthbound blocks of the laboratories.

Plans, from top
to bottom,
Roof level, Fourth level,
Second level.

Elimination of barriers
between offices and
between adjacent lab
modules was a major
goal for the planning of
the lab and office
wings. Floor to ceiling
glass at both the
inboard and outboard
walls enhances a sense
of community, with
views and natural light
shared by all.

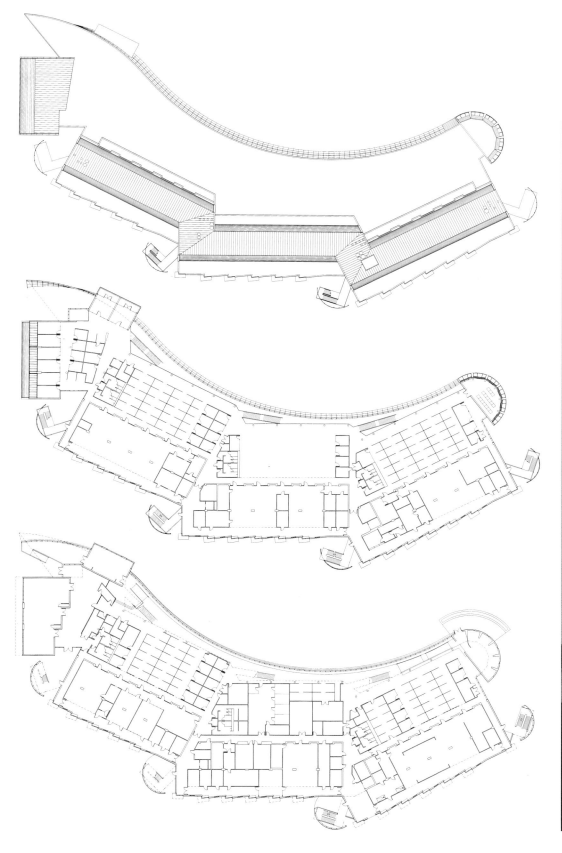

The north office elevation is a sweeping, sloped curved wall that wraps the building around the existing swale. There are outdoor patios at either end of the lobby.
Open spaces along the edge of the office area encourage interaction between two levels.

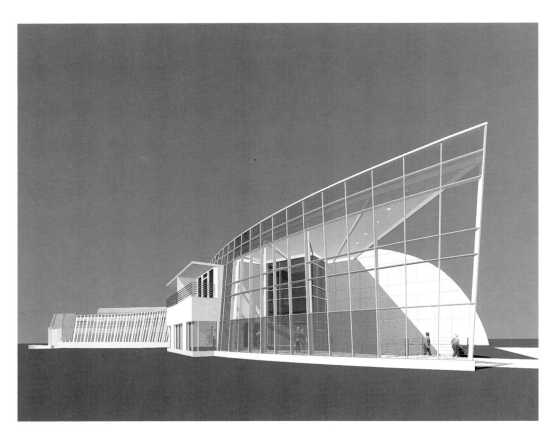

Williams College Unified Sciences Center
Williamstown, Massachusetts, 1999-2000

At present, the existing science facilities at Williams College are housed in four separate buildings: three Thompson Laboratories circa 1900 and the Bronfman Science Center circa 1968. One of the primary goals for this project is to increase the interdisciplinary nature of the science program at Williams by creating a unified science building. In doing so, it is important to respect the scale and quality of the main quad, the location of commencement ceremonies, and one of the most cherished places on the campus.

New construction includes a 79,000-square-foot laboratory building that will serve to connect the three existing science buildings, totaling 100,000 square feet, all of which will be renovated. The central space created by the new construction will house a 40,000-square-foot unified science library and Science Court.

The design capitalizes on the configuration of the existing buildings to create a library that is the physical center and hearth of the complex. Existing and new labs and classrooms are arranged around the library making it the academic focus of the science complex.

To foster the interdisciplinary approach to teaching science, interaction areas are located along the primary circulation path. These study areas open to the corridor and are equipped with blackboards, tables and furniture to encourage student interaction.

The main entrance to the facility, the Science Court, provides additional areas for exhibiting student and faculty research projects, and a coffee bar.

To maximize use of the existing facilities, the lab space is located in the new building. Office and support spaces are in the existing structures where flexibility in the mechanical systems is more limited.

The materials and color of the building addition are blended into the family of the existing buildings. The interior is seamless with the three older Thompson labs that will now house the less laboratory-intensive activities.

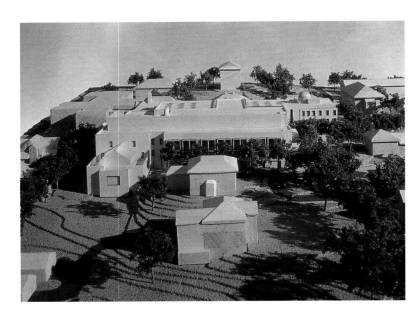

A major addition
to the science complex
integrates nine
departments in a
combination of new and
existing space at a scale
consistent with a
cherished part of this
historic campus.
From bottom left, plans,
counter-clockwise,
Ground floor, First floor,
Second floor, Third floor.

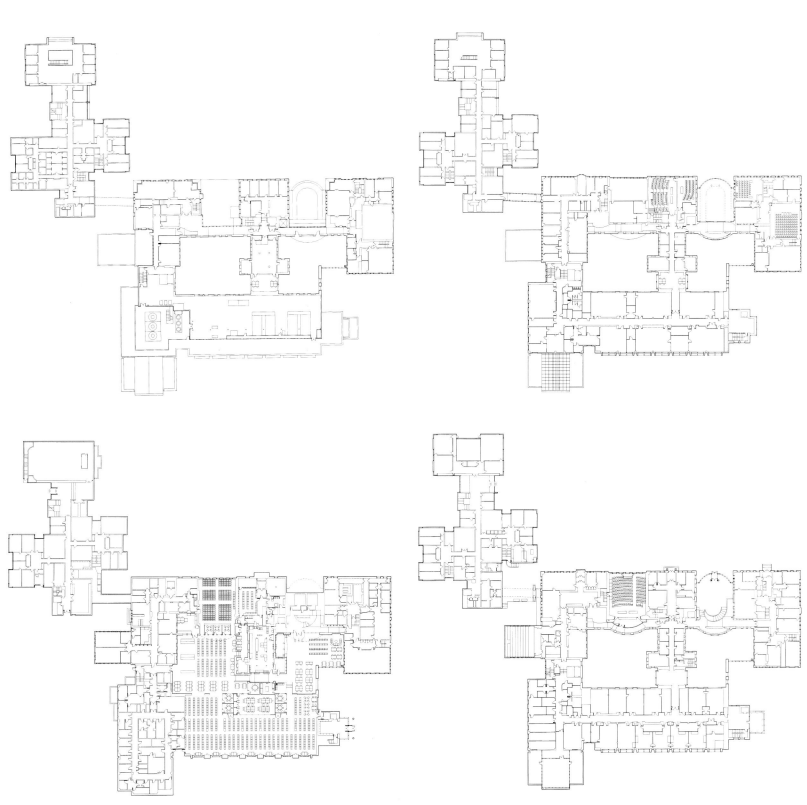

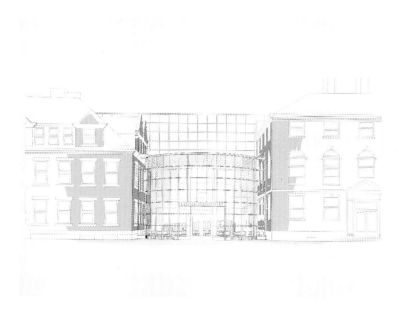

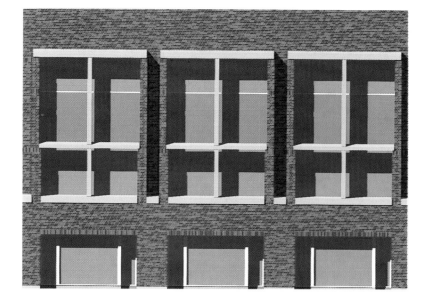

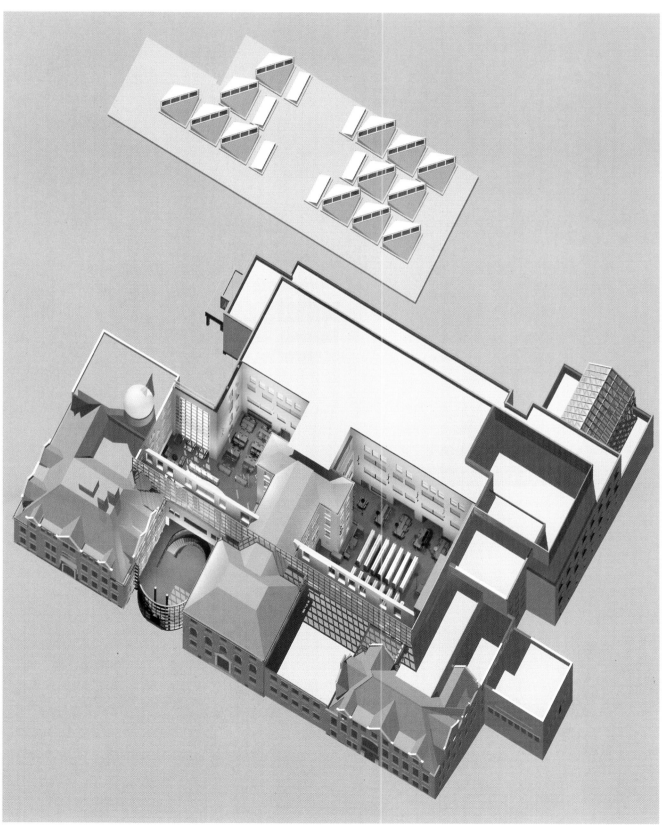

The hearth of the complex is a new unified science library, a skylit room that knits together the old and the new. A number of interaction spaces are organized around the perimeter of the library above.

Above left, the Science Court, as the only intervention in this fragile quad, is designed as a transparent building connection that allows the historic architecture of the neighboring buildings to remain pre-eminent in the composition of the quad.

SAFECO Redmond Campus
Redmond, Washington, 2000

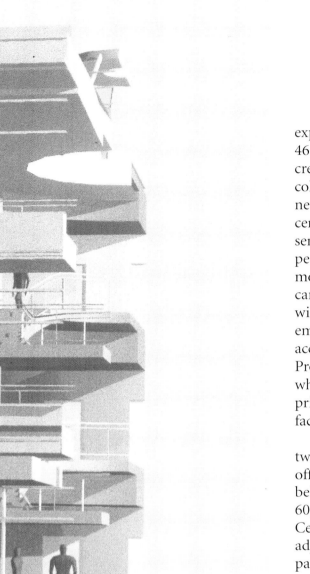

The plan for the extensive expansion and alteration of SAFECO's 46-acre headquarters campus will create a unified image and a more collegial campus environment. The new buildings are organized around a central "campus green" to establish a sense of community and to separate pedestrian traffic from vehicular movement. A new winding, central campus lane is being designed, which will be restricted to visitor and emergency traffic while staff parking is accessed via the perimeter road. Provisions for personal security of staff while on campus has been a high priority in the design of the campus facilities and infrastructure.

The expanded campus will include two 150,000-square-foot, three-story office buildings with two levels of below-grade parking for 820 cars; a 60,000-square-foot, two-level Data Center; a 500-seat cafeteria and adjacent conference center; a five-level parking garage for 720 cars; and a three-level below-grade garage for 460 cars.

At the heart of the campus green is the cafeteria with reflecting pond and adjacent state-of-the-art conference and meeting facilities. It is designed to encourage staff interaction by linking the campus office buildings to the cafeteria with covered walkways.

The majority of the building's exterior is enclosed with tall glass doors, permitting the inside to extend out to an adjacent dining terrace and reflecting pool. The tall windows also allow the cafeteria to act as a "lantern" to the campus on the dark cold days of winter. Inside, the multi-level room creates a variety of dining environments and permits unobstructed views out to the campus green and reflecting pond. The flexible building design allows for an intimate dining experience and yet comfortably accommodates campus-wide meetings.

The new office buildings have been designed to maximize flexibility as well as allow for departmental identity.

The building lobbies are designed to be inviting and welcoming to staff and visitors while providing security at each building. Graciously sized lobbies and stairs are filled with natural light, creating a pleasant work environment and encouraging interaction between staff.

The mass of the new office buildings and the design of the exterior wall have been carefully shaped and scaled. The introduction of arcades at the ground floor and upper level setbacks in the building facades diminish the apparent scale and allow the buildings to sit more comfortably in this more intimate campus environment.

Site planning for
the phased expansion
of the SAFECO
headquarters
is intended to create
a more humanistic
campus environment.
Buildings are organized
around a central green,
and connected with
covered walkways.

Exterior materials, including natural stone and copper, precast and cast-in-place concrete, were selected to harmonize with existing buildings and create a unified campus appearance.

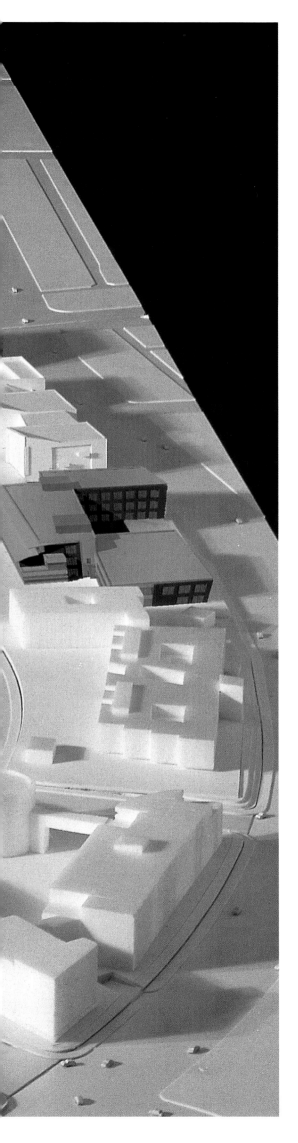

Entertainment, Media, Technology Building
Playa Vista, Los Angeles, California, 2000

One of the key components of the Playa Vista Master Plan is the Entertainment, Media, Technology District located on the 100-acre eastern portion of the property. The district is to be developed as a creative studio campus and production office environment for use by leading edge companies involved in the television and film industry. ZGF was commissioned by Maguire Partners to design this office building over two levels of underground parking as a part of an ensemble of office, retail and studio buildings by other noted architects.

The proposed building combines the industrial imagery and interior spatial qualities of the historic Howard Hughes Aircraft buildings that are currently located on the site, with the modern-day convenience and adaptability of a progressive office environment. This design approach builds upon the successful pattern of adaptive reuse of bow-string and similar utilitarian buildings into professional office space, blending character, identity and efficiency as an effective marketing tool. The design draws from two building types to create a balance between character and efficiency. First is the versatile loft building. This type of building embodies the essence of a production facility, where mezzanines overlook double-height, flexible work-areas.

On the exterior, the barrel roof expresses the interior volume and helps define the building's character. Second is the common office building.

This type of building is efficient due to its modular structural and architectural components, optimal bay proportions and simple perimeter walls.

Tenant identity is enhanced by private patios which flank the leased spaces on the plaza level. A tenant may choose to utilize their patio as an entry court or as an outdoor destination garden.

The proposed building provides significant leasing versatility by having large, contiguous floor plates. Also, the building massing allows a variety of demising options both horizontal and vertical to accommodate multiple tenants.

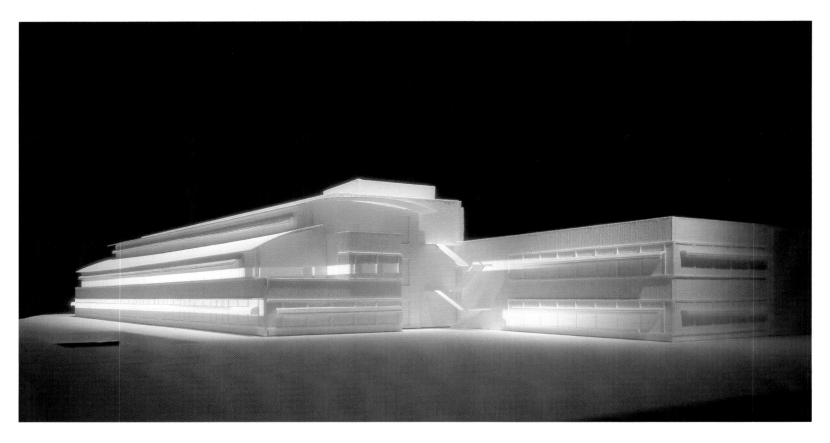

The architecture of the EMT references the industrial qualities of the historic aircraft buildings on the Playa Vista site. It draws upon two building types, the versatile loft building and the modern office building.
Right, Site plan.

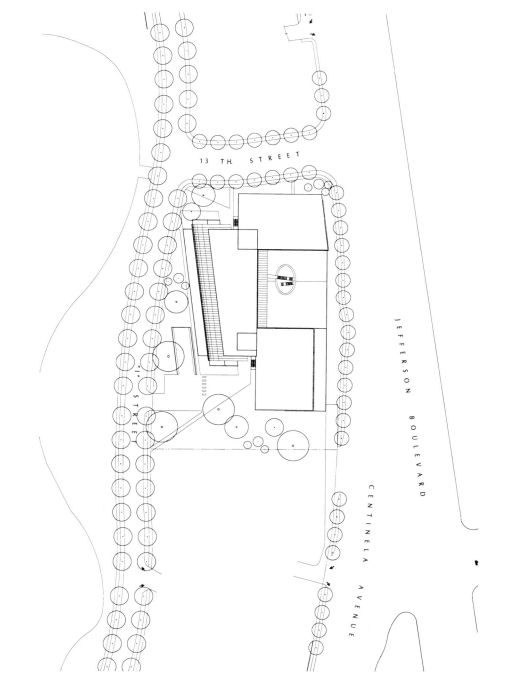

Two distinct industrial treatments are proposed for the exterior materials of the building. Ribbon metal windows project from corrugated metal siding on the south and west elevations. The south edge features the loft building type which bridges the two office wings. This building element is setback at an angle, opening the building interior to gardens.
Right, Ground floor plan.

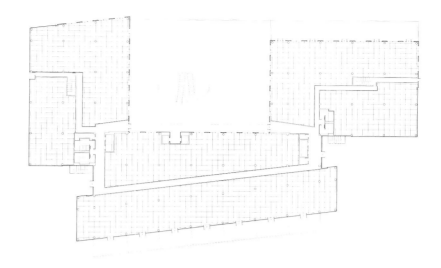

Assembly Building
The Church of Jesus Christ of Latter-day Saints
Salt Lake City, Utah, 2001

The program was to design an expanded assembly and performance facility to house functions previously accommodated in the Mormon Tabernacle, including the semiannual LDS General Conference and religious pageants.

The 1.1 million gross-square-foot Assembly Building complex will occupy an entire 10-acre city block adjacent to Temple Square in downtown Salt Lake City. The complex includes a 21,000-seat assembly room, a 1,000-seat regional theater, and a 1,400-car underground parking structure.

The assembly building contains an orchestra level seating 8,000, with mezzanine and balcony levels, each seating 6,500.

The principal urban design goal was to produce a solution that would honor the physical, historical and spiritual significance of the Temple and other buildings within Temple Square.

The intent of the architecture is to transform the building into landscape by creating a series of terraces that respond to the dramatically sloping site, and reflect the harmony and beauty of nature itself. The solution essentially doubles the size of the urban parklike quality of Temple Square; the terraces create a garden setting that enables the building to participate in the life of the city throughout the year.

The main entrance of the building is on the southeast corner of the block, facing the Joseph Smith Building and the main entrance to the Temple. At street level, the arrival sequence begins in a public, urban space.

A landscaped plaza, which focuses on the regional theater, is designed for ease of movement of large crowds of people to the orchestra level, as well as providing an amenity on a day-to-day basis.

Each of the three levels of the primary assembly building extends to the outdoors onto a continuous terrace that overlooks Temple Square. From atop the terraces, views are provided to the historic Temple and grounds.

A waterfall is situated on the axis of the Temple Square gardens. Exterior materials incorporate the same granite and glass used on the historic Temple.

The major interior room—the auditorium—is designed primarily as a worship space, but can accommodate performances with the back-stage infrastructure to support it. A key challenge was to provide strong visual connection to the rostrum, to build a sense of community and family with the congregation. State-of-the-art sound reinforcement systems have been designed to provide proper acoustics for voice and music within this large room. A sophisticated Early Reflected Energy System creates and controls the amount of reverberation to enhance the quality of music.

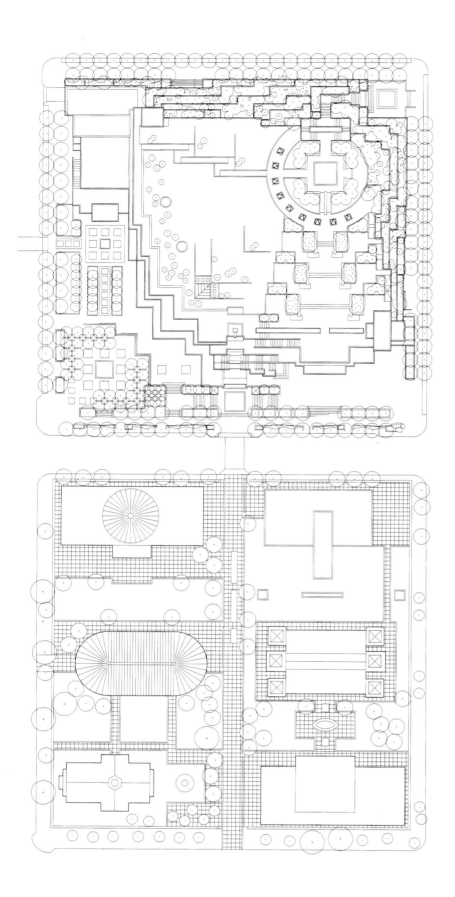

The site plan extends the spirit of Temple Square by doubling its size and continuing the landscape at street level and above the new Assembly Building.

The site for the Assembly Building slopes 60 feet diagonally, making it possible to easily access two of the main levels of the hall and roof garden at the northeast corner.

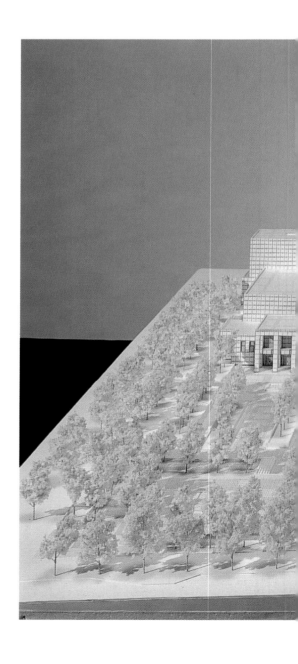

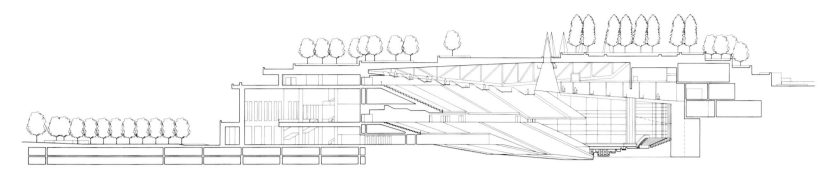

Left, the 21,000-seat performance hall features over 900 seats on the rostrum for the choir and church leadership. The hall is skylit from the roof garden above. Above left, North-South section.

Plans, below, First floor orchestra level, Second floor orchestra mezzanine level, Third floor terrace level.

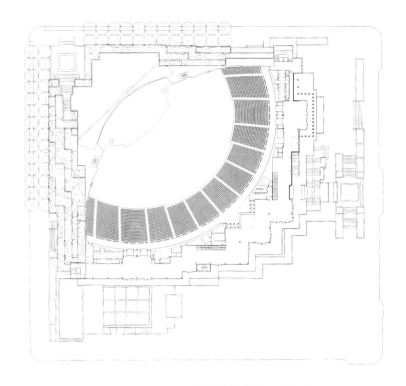

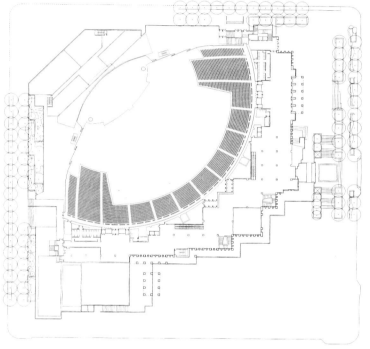

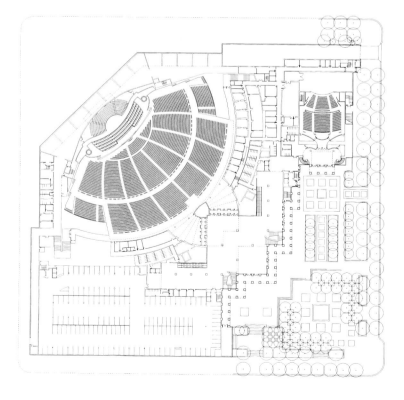

The central axis
of Temple Square
focuses on the waterfall
and stair access
to the roof garden.

Above, entrance to the 1,000-seat theatre and orchestra level of the Assembly Hall and focal point of the lower street level and courtyard. Below, North Temple Street facade which includes entrances to orchestra level and terrace level of the Assembly Hall.

Mark O. Hatfield Clinical Research Center National Institutes of Health, Bethesda, Maryland, 2002

This unique program is an 850,000-gross-square-foot addition to the Clinical Center on the Bethesda campus of the National Institutes of Health (NIH). The mix of components includes research laboratories, a 250-bed hospital, an outpatient clinic, NIH offices, and other common facilities. Each component requires a distinct identity while maintaining an appropriate relationship to the entire complex. Critical to the design of the new Clinical Research Center (CRC) is the proximity of laboratories to patient care. NIH has a tradition of rapidly moving scientific findings into mainstream medical practice, and the close relationship between laboratory and patient-care functions will continue and enhance this mission.

Another factor in the life of this expansion project is the role of the adjacent, 41-year-old existing Clinical Center. Direct connections and clear functional relationships between old and new facilities are important in order to functionally integrate as well as dignify the existing three million square foot building. The building must further reconcile 21st century technological requirements with the need to create a humane research and healing patient care environment.

The design proposes a low-rise structure of four brick wings, paired around landscaped courtyards, and flanking a glass-enclosed Science Court. This 10-story space provides a main gathering area and serves as the circulation hub of the complex. A double-helix stair—designed to recall the structure of a DNA molecule—serves as the defining element of the Science Court. Connecting all floors of the CRC at alternating quadrants, the stair hangs from trusses overhead,
allowing it to visually float and enhance the overall lightness of the space.

NIH offices connect the laboratories and patient care units, and serve as a focal point between the two. This location maximizes convenience, provides the opportunity for interaction, and gives each of the institutes their much desired identity. Both the laboratories and nursing units are designed for total flexibility, either within the unit or by allowing conversion from laboratory to patient unit and vice versa. An interstitial floor accommodates the distribution of all building systems, further enhancing the building's flexibility for future change.

A vertical circulation core wraps a portion of the existing building, covering a glass wall with a new brick facade. Relating to the brick used throughout the CRC as well as to that of the majority of NIH buildings, the new facade provides both a visual and functional connection between the new CRC, the existing building, and the rest of the NIH campus.

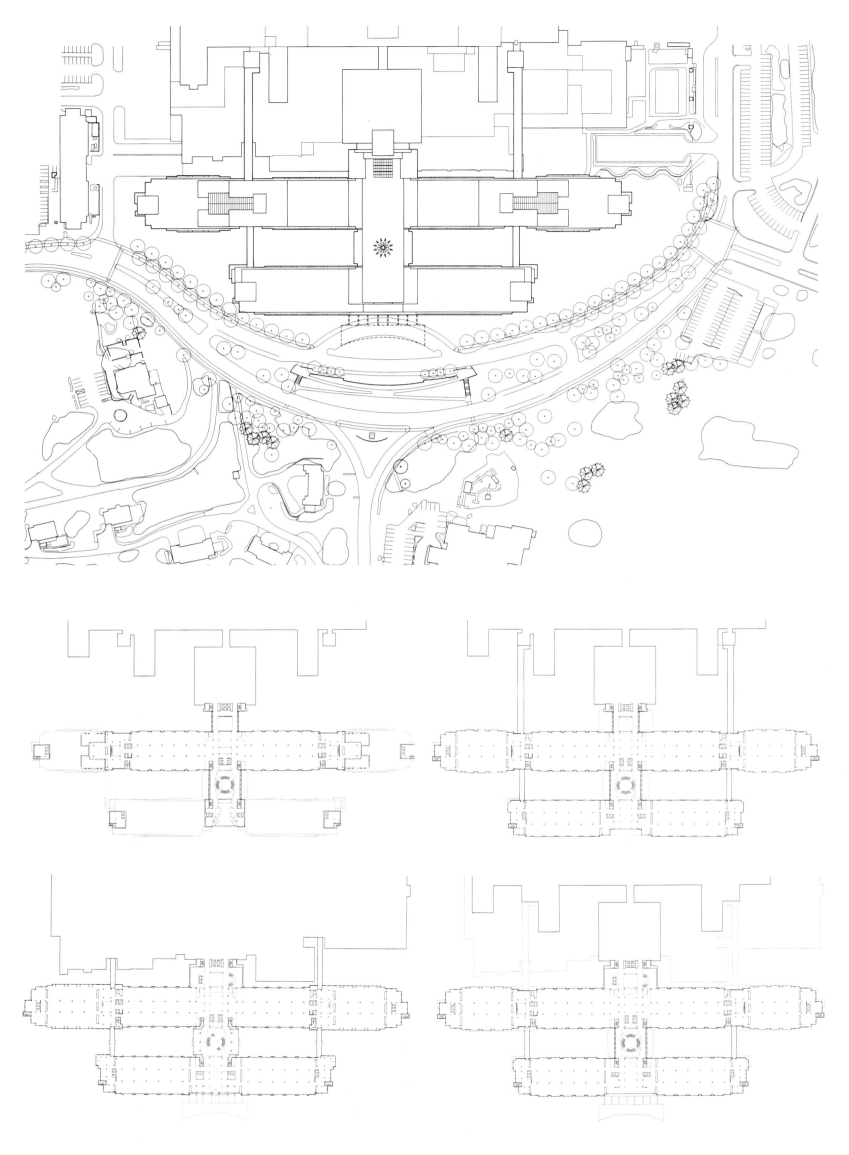

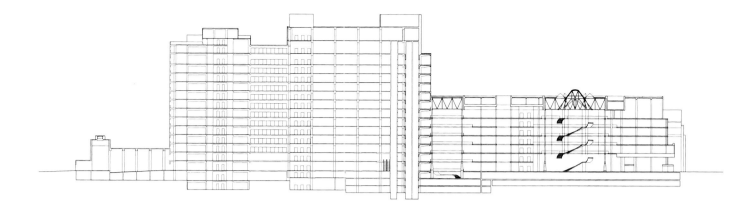

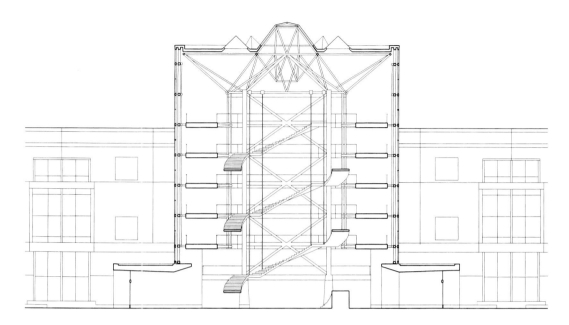

Left above, Site plan; below, from bottom left, plans, counter-clockwise, First floor, Third floor, Fifth floor, Seventh floor.

Above, North/South section. Right, Science Court section. Below, this project integrates an existing three-million-square-foot facility with an 850,000-square-foot addition of research labs and patient care and strives to inject the existing building with a new spirit.

Artist Larry Kirkland interviewed NIH scientists and is incorporating imagery from their work, in both pictorial and narrative form, into the double-helix stair, the focus of the Science Court.

The Science Court
serves as the principal
public room of the
Clinical Center complex.
Interaction is facilitated
by shared facilities such
as food service,
bookstore, and the
double helix stair that
connects every level
of the new and existing
facilities.

Chronology
of Selected Works

1975 - 1985
Tom McCall Waterfront Park Master
Plan and Phase I, Portland, Oregon

Benjamin Franklin Plaza, Portland, Oregon

Tektronix, Inc. Beaverton and Wilsonville
Campuses, Oregon

Tektronix, Inc. Clark County Campus,
Vancouver, Washington

Henry Failing Building, Portland, Oregon

Kah-Nee-Ta Vacation Resort,
Warm Springs, Oregon

Oregon State Capitol Building Wings Addition,
Salem, Oregon

World Trade Center, Portland, Oregon

Columbia Square, Portland, Oregon

Crown Plaza, Portland, Oregon

U.S. Embassy Addition, Vienna, Austria

Sherlock Building Renovation,
Portland, Oregon

Bonneville Lock and Dam Second
Powerhouse, The Dalles, Oregon

Justice Center, Portland, Oregon

Atwater's Restaurant, Portland, Oregon

KOIN Center, Olympia & York of
Oregon, Inc., Portland, Oregon

1986
RiverPlace Athletic Club, Portland, Oregon

Banfield Light Rail Transitway,
Portland, Oregon

St. Vincent Hospital and Medical Center Critical
Care Building Addition, Portland, Oregon

1987
Bonneville Power Administration Headquarters,
Portland, Oregon

Bank of America Financial Center, Portland,
Oregon

Vollum Institute, Oregon Health Sciences
University, Portland, Oregon

1988
The Link, Kansas City, Missouri

Whitman College Master Plan and Residence
Halls, Walla Walla, Washington

Sunset Presbyterian Church, Portland, Oregon

1989
Federal Correctional Institution,
Sheridan, Oregon

Delta Air Lines Concourse and Crown Room,
Portland International Airport, Portland, Oregon

Linfield College Physical Education & Athletic
Facility, McMinnville, Oregon

Reed College Hauser Library, Portland, Oregon

Oregon Historical Society, Portland, Oregon

1990
Oregon Convention Center, Portland, Oregon

Alsea Bay Bridge, Waldport, Oregon

1991
Oregon State Archives, Salem, Oregon

Hewlett Packard Vancouver Division
Building 2, Vancouver, Washington

The Master Plan for the Capitol of the State of
Washington, Olympia, Washington

Northgate Transit Center, Seattle, Washington

Robert Duncan Plaza, Portland, Oregon

Second & Seneca Office Building, Seattle,
Washington

1992
Exposition Park Master Plan, Los Angeles,
California

Willamette University Goudy
Commons, Salem, Oregon

Sunset Corporate Campus, Bellevue, Washington

Reed College Chemistry Building, Portland,
Oregon

Oregon Museum of Science and Industry,
Portland, Oregon

1993
Temple Beth Israel Expansion, Portland, Oregon

Fred Hutchinson Cancer Research Center, Phase
I, Seattle, Washington

Bellevue Regional Library, Bellevue, Washington

St. Vincent Hospital and Medical Center, West
Pavilion, Portland, Oregon

Reed College Psychology Building, Portland,
Oregon

1994
Olympia Medical Center, Group Health
Cooperative of Puget Sound, Olympia,
Washington

Portland International Airport Terminal
Expansion North, Portland, Oregon

Portland Transit Mall Extension, Portland,
Oregon

Pacific Medical Center Tower Addition and
Renovation, Seattle, Washington

Engineering Building Unit II, University of
California, San Diego, California

Engineering Unit 2, University of California,
Irvine, California

University of Alaska Westridge Natural Science
Facility, Fairbanks, Alaska

Washington State University Holland Library,
Pullman, Washington

Earth & Marine Sciences Building, University of
California, Santa Cruz, California

1995
Kirkland Library, Kirkland, Washington

Pacific Lutheran University Mary Baker
Russell Music Center, Tacoma, Washington

Peninsula Center Library Addition and
Renovation, Palos Verdes Peninsula, California

River District Development Plan, Portland,
Oregon

16th Street Mall Extension, Denver, Colorado

Western Washington University Biology
Building, Bellingham, Washington

University of Southern California Katherine
Bogdanovich Wing, Loker Hydrocarbon
Institute, Los Angeles, California

1996
Bothell Library, Bothell, Washington

Fifth Avenue Suites Hotel, Portland, Oregon

Microsoft Redmond West Campus, Redmond,
Washington

KPTV Studios and Headquarters, Portland,
Oregon

Washington State University Phase I Campus
Development, Vancouver, Washington

Western Washington University Science,
Mathematics and Technology Education Center,
Bellingham, Washington

Humanities and Social Sciences Complex,
University of California, Santa Barbara,
California

Life Sciences Building Addition, University of
California, Davis, California

1997
Monaco Hotel, Seattle, Washington

Microsoft Studios, Redmond,
Washington

Microsoft Pebble Beach, Redmond, Washington

William R. Wiley Environmental Molecular
Sciences Laboratory, U. S. Department of Energy,
Richland, Washington

Reed College Gray Campus Center, Portland,
Oregon

Oregon State University West International House and Marketplace West, Corvallis, Oregon

1998
California Science Center, Los Angeles, California

Washington County Justice Complex, Hillsboro, Oregon

Ronald Reagan Federal Building and US Courthouse, Santa Ana, California

International District Village Square, Seattle, Washington

Portland International Airport Terminal Expansion South, Phase I, Portland, Oregon

Westside Corridor Light Rail Project, Portland, Oregon

Hudson-Bergen Light Rail Transit System, New Jersey

Microsoft St. Andrews, Redmond, Washington

Fred Hutchinson Cancer Research Center, Phase II, Seattle, Washington

Amgen Building 29 Biotechnology Research Center, Thousand Oaks, California

Mark O. Hatfield Research Center, Oregon Health Sciences University, Portland, Oregon

Doernbecher Children's Hospital, Portland, Oregon

Reed College Bragdon Hall, Portland, Oregon

1999
Green Hill School Expansion and Rehabilitation, Chehalis, Washington

Portland International Airport Terminal Roadway and Parking Expansion, Portland, Oregon

World Trade Center, Port of Seattle/Wright Runstad & Company, Seattle, Washington

Port of Portland Headquarters Building, Portland, Oregon

ODS Tower, Portland, Oregon

Laboratory and Animal Facility, National Institute of Biologicals, Noida, Uttar Pradesh, India

St. Vincent Medical Office Building IV and Parking Structure, Portland, Oregon

Johns Hopkins University, Cancer Research Building, Baltimore, Maryland

University of Southern California Ralph and Goldy Lewis Hall, School of Urban Planning and Development, Los Angeles, California

Willamette University Music Center, Salem, Oregon

2000
Assembly Building Complex, The Church of Jesus Christ of Latter-day Saints, Salt Lake City, Utah

Everett Multi-modal Transportation Center, Everett, Washington

Safeco Insurance Company Redmond Campus Expansion, Redmond, Washington

Millennium Tower, Seattle, Washington

University of Texas M.D. Anderson Cancer Center Research Facility Addition, Houston, Texas

University of Puget Sound Academic Building 2000, Tacoma, Washington

Williams College Unified Sciences Center, Williamstown, Massachusetts

2001
FDA at Irvine, Irvine, California

Cancer Care Alliance Outpatient Facility, Seattle, Washington

Northwestern University Life Science/CEAR Building, Evanston, Illinois

Northwestern University Center for Nanofabrication and Molecular Self-Assembly, Evanston, Illinois

Ohio State University Physical Sciences Research Building, Columbus, Ohio

Cornell University Duffield Hall, Advanced Science & Technology Initiative, Ithaca, New York

Donald Bren School of Environmental Science and Management / Marine Sciences Institute, University of California, Santa Barbara, California

2002
National Institutes of Health Mark O. Hatfield Clinical Research Center, Bethesda, Maryland

Credits

Bellevue Regional Library
Bellevue, Washington

1997 AIA National Honor Award
1995 AIA Merit Award, Pacific and Northwest Region
1995 ALA/AIA National Award of Excellence for Library Architecture
1994 AIA Honor Award, Portland Chapter
1993 AIA Award of Merit, Seattle Chapter

Client: King County Library System
Artists: Richard S. Beyer, Garth Edwards
Paul Marioni, Sepp Mayrhuber, Hisashi Otsuka, Ann Storrs, Ann Troutner, Walter White
Photographers: Timothy Hursley, Strode Eckert Photographic

Peninsula Center Library
Palos Verdes Peninsula, Rolling Hills Estates, California
1996 AIA Award of Merit, Cabrillo Chapter
1996 AIA/ASID/IIDA Honor Award, Portland Chapters

Client: Palos Verdes Library District
Artists: Lita Albuquerque, Gwynne Murrill
Photographer: Nick Merrick/Hedrich Blessing

High Technology Corporate Campus Cafeteria
Redmond, Washington

1997 AIA Award of Merit, Northwest & Pacific Region
1996 AIA Award of Merit, Seattle Chapter

Landscape Architects: Murase Associates, Brumbaugh & Associates
Photographer: Nick Merrick/Hedrich Blessing

Humanities and Social Sciences Building
University of California, Santa Barbara, California

1992 AIA Honorable Mention, Orange County Chapter

Client: University of California, Santa Barbara
Photographers: Nick Merrick/Hedrich Blessing, Anthony Peres

Reed College Gray Campus Center
Portland, Oregon

Client: Reed College
Photographer: Eckert & Eckert

William R. Wiley Environmental Molecular Sciences Laboratory
Richland, Washington

1998 Lab of the Year Special Mention Award, R & D Magazine

Client: US Department of Energy/Pacific Northwest National Laboratory
Photographers: Timothy Hursley, PNNL/Lockheed Martin Services Inc., Strode Eckert Photographic

California Science Center
Los Angeles, California

1998 AIA Citation Award, Portland Chapter
1993 AIA Award of Merit, Orange County Chapter
1993 AIA National Urban Design Award of Excellence

Client: California Science Center, State of California
Artists: Hoberman Associates, Larry Kirkland Studios
Consulting Architect: RAW International
Consulting Historical Architect: Offenhauser/Mekeel Architects
Exhibition Designer: West Office Exhibition Design
Photographers: Timothy Hursley, Mark Schwartz, Adrian Velicescu

Doernbecher Children's Hospital
Portland, Oregon

Client: Oregon Health Sciences University
Artists: Laura Bender, Frank Boyden, Wayne Chabre, Fernanda D'Agostino, John Earley, Jim Hirschfield, Sonya Ishii, Suzanne Lee, Valerie Otani, Brad Rude, Kim Stafford, Elizabeth Stanek, Margot Thompson
Associate Architect/Health Care Planners: Anshen + Allen
Photographers: Timothy Hursley, Eckert & Eckert

Westside Light Rail Corridor
Portland, Oregon

1998 AIA Honor Award, Portland Chapter

Client: Tri-Met
Core Artists: Norie Sato, Tad Savinar, Richard Turner, Mierle Ukeles, Bill Will
Core Design Team: Parsons Brinckerhoff Quade & Douglas, Inc., BRW Inc., LTK Engineering Services, OTAK, Inc.
Landscape Architect: Murase Associates
Information/Communications: Mayer/Reed
Photographers: Eckert & Eckert, C. Bruce Forster, Strode Photographic LLC

Portland International Airport Terminal Access Program,
Portland, Oregon

Client: Port of Portland
Civil Engineer, Terminal Planner & Parking Consultant: HNTB Corp.
Photographer: Strode Eckert Photographic

ODS Tower
Portland, Oregon

Client: Wright Runstad & Company, ODS Health Plan
Artist: Judy Pfaff
Photographer: Eckert & Eckert

US Food Drug Administration
Irvine, California

Client: US Food and Drug Administration
Joint Venture Partner: Henningson, Durham & Richardson, Inc.
Photographers: Wayne Thom Photographer, Adrian Velicescu

Williams College Unified Sciences Center
Williamstown, Massachusetts

Client: Williams College
Executive Architect: Einhorn Yaffee Prescott
Photographer: Strode Eckert Photographic

SAFECO Redmond Campus
Redmond, Washington

Client: SAFECO Insurance Companies
Photographer: Chris J. Roberts

Entertainment, Media, Technology Building
Playa Vista, Los Angeles, California

Owner: Playa Capital Group
Developer: Maguire Partners
Photographer: Adrian Velicescu

Assembly Building
Salt Lake City, Utah

Client: The Church of Jesus Christ of Latter-day Saints
Consulting Architects: Lee Gray, The Church of Jesus Christ of Latter-day Saints Gillies Stransky Brems Smith Architects
Landscape Architect: The Olin Partnership
Theatre Consultant: Auerbach + Associates
Lighting Design: Auerbach + Glasow
Photographer: Strode Photographic LLC

Mark O. Hatfield Clinical Research Center
Bethesda, Maryland

Client: National Institutes of Health
Artist: Larry Kirkland Studios
Health Care Programmers/Planners: NBBJ
Laboratory Planners: Walls/Copenhagen
Landscape Architect: EDAW, Inc.
Photographer: Eckert & Eckert